MznLnx

Missing Links Exam Preps

Exam Prep for

Internet Marketing and e-Commerce

Hanson & Kalyanam, 1st Edition

The MznLnx Exam Prep is your link from the texbook and lecture to your exams.
The MznLnx Exam Preps are unauthorized and comprehensive reviews of your textbooks.

All material provided by MznLnx and Rico Publications (c) 2010
Textbook publishers and textbook authors do not particpate in or contribute to these reviews.

MznLnx

Rico Publications

Exam Prep for Internet Marketing and e-Commerce
1st Edition
Hanson & Kalyanam

Publisher: Raymond Houge
Assistant Editor: Michael Rouger
Text and Cover Designer: Lisa Buckner
Marketing Manager: Sara Swagger
Project Manager, Editorial Production: Jerry Emerson
Art Director: Vernon Lowerui

Product Manager: Dave Mason
Editorial Assitant: Rachel Guzmanji
Pedagogy: Debra Long
Cover Image: Jim Reed/Getty Images
Text and Cover Printer: City Printing, Inc.
Compositor: Media Mix, Inc.

(c) 2010 Rico Publications
ALL RIGHTS RESERVED. No part of this work covered by the copyright may be reproduced or used in any form or by an means--graphic, electronic, or mechanical, including photocopying, recording, taping, Web distribution, information storage, and retrieval systems, or in any other manner--without the written permission of the publisher.

Printed in the United States
ISBN:

For more information about our products, contact us at:
Dave.Mason@RicoPublications.com

For permission to use material from this text or product, submit a request online to:
Dave.Mason@RicoPublications.com

Contents

CHAPTER 1
Introduction — 1

CHAPTER 2
A Digital World — 11

CHAPTER 3
Networks — 16

CHAPTER 4
Individuals Online — 23

CHAPTER 5
Web Business Models — 29

CHAPTER 6
Online Branding — 36

CHAPTER 7
Usability, Credibility, and Persuasion — 44

CHAPTER 8
Traffic Building — 50

CHAPTER 9
Personalization — 59

CHAPTER 10
Creating Commitment — 68

CHAPTER 11
Innovation and the Net — 73

CHAPTER 12
Pricing in an Online World — 79

CHAPTER 13
Internet Retailing — 85

CHAPTER 14
Consumer Channels — 91

CHAPTER 15
B2B e-Commerce — 100

CHAPTER 16
Online Research — 107

CHAPTER 17
Organizing for Online Marketing — 113

ANSWER KEY — 120

TO THE STUDENT

COMPREHENSIVE

The *MznLnx* Exam Prep series is designed to help you pass your exams. Editors at MznLnx review your textbooks and then prepare these practice exams to help you master the textbook material. Unlike study guides, workbooks, and practice tests provided by the texbook publisher and textbook authors, *MznLnx* gives you **all** of the material in each chapter in exam form, not just samples, so you can be sure to nail your exam.

MECHANICAL

The MznLnx Exam Prep series creates exams that will help you learn the subject matter as well as test you on your understanding. Each question is designed to help you master the concept. Just working through the exams, you gain an understanding of the subject--its a simple mechanical process that produces success.

INTEGRATED STUDY GUIDE AND REVIEW

MznLnx is not just a set of exams designed to test you, its also a comprehensive review of the subject content. Each exam question is also a review of the concept, making sure that you will get the answer correct without having to go to other sources of material. You learn as you go! Its the easiest way to pass an exam.

HUMOR

Studying can be tedious and dry. MznLnx's instructional design includes moderate humor within the exam questions on occassion, to break the tedium and revitalize the brain

Chapter 1. Introduction

1. _____ is Google's flagship advertising product and main source of revenue ($21 billion in 2008.) _____ offers pay-per-click (PPC) advertising, and site-targeted advertising for both text and banner ads. The _____ program includes local, national, and international distribution.
   a. AMAX
   b. ACNielsen
   c. AdWords
   d. ADTECH

2. A _____ is a collection of symbols, experiences and associations connected with a product, a service, a person or any other artifact or entity.

   _____s have become increasingly important components of culture and the economy, now being described as 'cultural accessories and personal philosophies'.

   Some people distinguish the psychological aspect of a _____ from the experiential aspect.

   a. Brand equity
   b. Brand
   c. Store brand
   d. Brandable software

3. _____, also referred to as i-marketing, web marketing, online marketing is the marketing of products or services over the Internet.

   The Internet has brought many unique benefits to marketing, one of which being lower costs for the distribution of information and media to a global audience. The interactive nature of _____, both in terms of providing instant response and eliciting responses, is a unique quality of the medium.

   a. ADTECH
   b. Internet marketing
   c. ACNielsen
   d. AMAX

4. _____ is defined by the American _____ Association as the activity, set of institutions, and processes for creating, communicating, delivering, and exchanging offerings that have value for customers, clients, partners, and society at large. The term developed from the original meaning which referred literally to going to market, as in shopping, or going to a market to sell goods or services.

   _____ practice tends to be seen as a creative industry, which includes advertising, distribution and selling.

Chapter 1. Introduction

a. Customer acquisition management
b. Marketing myopia
c. Product naming
d. Marketing

5. The _____ is a very large set of interlinked hypertext documents accessed via the Internet. With a Web browser, one can view Web pages that may contain text, images, videos, and other multimedia and navigate between them using hyperlinks. Using concepts from earlier hypertext systems, the _____ was begun in 1992 by the English physicist Sir Tim Berners-Lee, now the Director of the _____ Consortium, and Robert Cailliau, a Belgian computer scientist, while both were working at CERN in Geneva, Switzerland.
   a. 6-3-5 Brainwriting
   b. Power III
   c. World Wide Web
   d. 180SearchAssistant

6. _____ is a process by which government's control over businesses and individuals is reduced or eliminated. It is the removal of some governmental controls over a market. _____ does not mean elimination of laws against fraud, but eliminating or reducing government control of how business is done, thereby moving toward a more free market.
   a. Value added
   b. Consumer spending
   c. Power III
   d. Deregulation

7. _____ is difficult to define. For example, in 1952, Alfred Kroeber and Clyde Kluckhohn compiled a list of 164 definitions of '_____' in _____: A Critical Review of Concepts and Definitions. However, the word '_____' is most commonly used in three basic senses:

- excellence of taste in the fine arts and humanities
- an integrated pattern of human knowledge, belief, and behavior that depends upon the capacity for symbolic thought and social learning
- the set of shared attitudes, values, goals, and practices that characterizes an institution, organization or group.

When the concept first emerged in eighteenth- and nineteenth-century Europe, it connoted a process of cultivation or improvement, as in agriculture or horticulture. In the nineteenth century, it came to refer first to the betterment or refinement of the individual, especially through education, and then to the fulfillment of national aspirations or ideals.

Chapter 1. Introduction 3

   a. Albert Einstein
   b. AStore
   c. Culture
   d. African Americans

8. _____ is a market coverage strategy in which a firm decides to ignore market segment differences and go after the whole market with one offer.it is type of marketing (or attempting to sell through persuasion) of a product to a wide audience. The idea is to broadcast a message that will reach the largest number of people possible. Traditionally _____ has focused on radio, television and newspapers as the medium used to reach this broad audience.
   a. Cyberdoc
   b. Marketspace
   c. Mass marketing
   d. Business-to-consumer

9. _____ in economics and business is the result of an exchange and from that trade we assign a numerical monetary value to a good, service or asset. If I trade 4 apples for an orange, the _____ of an orange is 4 - apples. Inversely, the _____ of an apple is 1/4 oranges.
   a. Pricing
   b. Discounts and allowances
   c. Contribution margin-based pricing
   d. Price

10. _____ is an advertisement in which a particular product specifically mentions a competitor by name for the express purpose of showing why the competitor is inferior to the product naming it.

This should not be confused with parody advertisements, where a fictional product is being advertised for the purpose of poking fun at the particular advertisement, nor should it be confused with the use of a coined brand name for the purpose of comparing the product without actually naming an actual competitor. ('Wikipedia tastes better and is less filling than the Encyclopedia Galactica.')

In the 1980s, during what has been referred to as the cola wars, soft-drink manufacturer Pepsi ran a series of advertisements where people, caught on hidden camera, in a blind taste test, chose Pepsi over rival Coca-Cola.

   a. Heavy-up
   b. Cost per conversion
   c. GL-70
   d. Comparative advertising

11. A _____ is an entity that provides services to other entities. Usually this refers to a business that provides subscription or web service to other businesses or individuals. Examples of these services include Internet access, Mobile phone operator, and web application hosting.

   a. Yield management
   b. Service provider
   c. Cross-selling
   d. Freebie marketing

12. _____ is the suppression of speech or deletion of communicative material which may be considered objectionable, harmful, sensitive, or inconvenient to the government or media organizations as determined by a censor.

The rationale for _____ is different for various types of information censored:

- Moral _____, is the removal of materials that are obscene or otherwise morally questionable. Pornography, for example, is often censored under this rationale, especially child pornography, which is censored in most jurisdictions in the world.
- Military _____ is the process of keeping military intelligence and tactics confidential and away from the enemy. This is used to counter espionage, which is the process of gleaning military information. Very often, militaries will also attempt to suppress politically inconvenient information even if that information has no actual intelligence value.
- Political _____ occurs when governments hold back information from their citizens. The logic is to exert control over the populace and prevent free expression that might foment rebellion.
- Religious _____ is the means by which any material objectionable to a certain faith is removed. This often involves a dominant religion forcing limitations on less prevalent ones. Alternatively, one religion may shun the works of another when they believe the content is not appropriate for their faith.
- Corporate _____ is the process by which editors in corporate media outlets intervene to halt the publishing of information that portrays their business or business partners in a negative light.

Strict _____ existed in the Eastern Bloc. Throughout the bloc, the various ministries of culture held a tight reign on their writers. Cultural products there reflected the propaganda needs of the state.

   a. Power III
   b. 180SearchAssistant
   c. 6-3-5 Brainwriting
   d. Censorship

13. _____ refers to any advertising that is linked to specific words or phrases. Common forms of _____ are known by many other terms including pay per click (PPC) and cost per action (CPA.) There are multiple variations each starting with 'pay per' or 'cost per' such as pay per action (PPA), pay per cost (PPC), cost per mille (CPM.)

Chapter 1. Introduction

a. Hover ads
b. Semantic targeting
c. Search advertising
d. Keyword advertising

14. _____. People may not recognize the value in offered personalization, such as when firms offer to customize product offers. Many people don't want to receive any such offers, period.

a. Little value placed on potential benefits
b. Push
c. Bottling lines
d. Category Development Index

15. _____ is a form of Internet marketing that seeks to promote websites by increasing their visibility in search engine result pages (SERPs.) According to the _____ Professional Organization, _____ methods include: search engine optimization (or SEO), paid placement, contextual advertising, and paid inclusion. Other sources, including the New York Times, define _____ as the practice of buying paid search listings.

a. Display advertising
b. Blog marketing
c. Pay for placement
d. Search engine marketing

16. _____ is a form of communication that typically attempts to persuade potential customers to purchase or to consume more of a particular brand of product or service. 'While now central to the contemporary global economy and the reproduction of global production networks, it is only quite recently that _____ has been more than a marginal influence on patterns of sales and production. The formation of modern _____ was intimately bound up with the emergence of new forms of monopoly capitalism around the end of the 19th and beginning of the 20th century as one element in corporate strategies to create, organize and where possible control markets, especially for mass produced consumer goods.

a. Advertising
b. ADTECH
c. AMAX
d. ACNielsen

17. _____ consists of the sale of goods or merchandise from a fixed location, such as a department store or kiosk in small or individual lots for direct consumption by the purchaser. _____ may include subordinated services, such as delivery. Purchasers may be individuals or businesses.

a. Thrifting
b. Warehouse store
c. Retailing
d. Charity shop

18. A _____ is a type of website, usually maintained by an individual with regular entries of commentary, descriptions of events, or other material such as graphics or video. Entries are commonly displayed in reverse-chronological order. '_____' can also be used as a verb, meaning to maintain or add content to a _____.
    a. 180SearchAssistant
    b. Power III
    c. 6-3-5 Brainwriting
    d. Blog

19. The term _____ is primarily used by mass media to describe any form of synchronous conferencing, occasionally even asynchronous conferencing. The term can thus mean any technology ranging from real-time online chat over instant messaging and online forums to fully immersive graphical social environments.

Online chat is a way of communicating by sending text messages to people in the same chat-room in real-time.

    a. Power III
    b. 180SearchAssistant
    c. 6-3-5 Brainwriting
    d. Chat room

20. _____ networking is a method of delivering computer network services in which the participants share a portion of their own resources, such as processing power, disk storage, network bandwidth, printing facilities. Such resources are provided directly to other participants without intermediary network hosts or servers. _____ network participants are providers and consumers of network services simultaneously, which contrasts with other service models, such as traditional client-server computing.
    a. 180SearchAssistant
    b. 6-3-5 Brainwriting
    c. Power III
    d. Peer-to-peer

Chapter 1. Introduction

21. _____ in organizations and public policy is both the organizational process of creating and maintaining a plan; and the psychological process of thinking about the activities required to create a desired goal on some scale. As such, it is a fundamental property of intelligent behavior. This thought process is essential to the creation and refinement of a plan, or integration of it with other plans, that is, it combines forecasting of developments with the preparation of scenarios of how to react to them.
   a. Power III
   b. Planning
   c. 6-3-5 Brainwriting
   d. 180SearchAssistant

22. _____ is the application of marketing techniques to a specific product, product line, or brand. It seeks to increase the product's perceived value to the customer and thereby increase brand franchise and brand equity. Marketers see a brand as an implied promise that the level of quality people have come to expect from a brand will continue with future purchases of the same product.
   a. Store brand
   b. Trademark distinctiveness
   c. Naming rights
   d. Brand management

23. In economics, _____ is the desire to own something and the ability to pay for it. The term _____ signifies the ability or the willingness to buy a particular commodity at a given point of time.

   a. Market dominance
   b. Discretionary spending
   c. Demand
   d. Market system

24. An _____ is a special-purpose computer system designed to perform one or a few dedicated functions, often with real-time computing constraints. It is usually embedded as part of a complete device including hardware and mechanical parts. In contrast, a general-purpose computer, such as a personal computer, can do many different tasks depending on programming.
   a. ACNielsen
   b. AMAX
   c. Embedded system
   d. ADTECH

25. The loyalty business model is a business model used in strategic management in which company resources are employed so as to increase the loyalty of customers and other stakeholders in the expectation that corporate objectives will be met or surpassed. A typical example of this type of model is: quality of product or service leads to customer satisfaction, which leads to _____, which leads to profitability.

Fredrick Reichheld (1996) expanded the loyalty business model beyond customers and employees.

   a. Power III
   b. Customer loyalty
   c. 6-3-5 Brainwriting
   d. 180SearchAssistant

26. On an intranet or B2E Enterprise Web portals, personalization is often based on user attributes such as department, functional area, or role. The term _____ in this context refers to the ability of users to modify the page layout or specify what content should be displayed.

There are two categories of personalizations:

   1. Rule-based
   2. Content-based

Web personalization models include rules-based filtering, based on 'if this, then that' rules processing, and collaborative filtering, which serves relevant material to customers by combining their own personal preferences with the preferences of like-minded others. Collaborative filtering works well for books, music, video, etc.

   a. Cashmere Agency
   b. Self branding
   c. Customization
   d. Movin'

27. _____ is a sub-discipline and type of marketing. There are two main definitional characteristics which distinguish it from other types of marketing. The first is that it attempts to send its messages directly to consumers, without the use of intervening media.
   a. Direct Marketing Associations
   b. Database marketing
   c. Direct marketing
   d. Power III

Chapter 1. Introduction

28. _____, in marketing, manufacturing, and management, is the use of flexible computer-aided manufacturing systems to produce custom output. Those systems combine the low unit costs of mass production processes with the flexibility of individual customization.

'_____' is the new frontier in business competition for both manufacturing and service industries.

   a. Flanking marketing warfare strategies
   b. Vertical integration
   c. Power III
   d. Mass customization

29. _____ or personalisation is tailoring a consumer product, electronic or written medium to a user based on personal details or characteristics they provide. More recently, it has especially been applied in the context of the World Wide Web.

Web pages are personalized based on the interests of an individual.

   a. Flighting
   b. Complex sale
   c. Sexism,
   d. Personalization

30. A _____ is a structured collection of records or data that is stored in a computer system. The structure is achieved by organizing the data according to a _____ model. The model in most common use today is the relational model.
   a. 180SearchAssistant
   b. 6-3-5 Brainwriting
   c. Power III
   d. Database

31. A personal and cultural _____ is a relative ethic _____, an assumption upon which implementation can be extrapolated. A _____ system is a set of consistent _____s and measures that is soo not true. A principle _____ is a foundation upon which other _____s and measures of integrity are based.
   a. Supreme Court of the United States
   b. Package-on-Package
   c. Perceptual maps
   d. Value

32. In marketing, customer _____, lifetime customer value (LCV), or _____ (LTV) and a new concept of 'customer life cycle management' is the present value of the future cash flows attributed to the customer relationship. Use of customer _____ as a marketing metric tends to place greater emphasis on customer service and long-term customer satisfaction, rather than on maximizing short-term sales.

Customer _____ has intuitive appeal as a marketing concept, because in theory it represents exactly how much each customer is worth in monetary terms, and therefore exactly how much a marketing department should be willing to spend to acquire each customer.

   a. Lifetime value
   b. Value chain
   c. Sweepstakes
   d. Brand infiltration

33. A _____ is a subgroup of people or organizations sharing one or more characteristics that cause them to have similar product and/or service needs. A true _____ meets all of the following criteria: it is distinct from other segments (different segments have different needs), it is homogeneous within the segment (exhibits common needs); it responds similarly to a market stimulus, and it can be reached by a market intervention. The term is also used when consumers with identical product and/or service needs are divided up into groups so they can be charged different amounts.
   a. Production orientation
   b. Commercial planning
   c. Market segment
   d. Customer insight

34. _____ is the practice of promoting products and services using digital distribution channels to reach consumers in a timely, relevant, personal and cost-effective manner.

Whilst _____ does include many of the techniques and practices contained within the category of Internet Marketing, it extends beyond this by including other channels with which to reach people that do not require the use of The Internet. As a result of this non-reliance on the Internet, the field of _____ includes a whole host of elements such as mobile phones, sms/mms, display / banner ads and digital outdoor.

   a. Diversity marketing
   b. Relationship marketing
   c. Global marketing
   d. Digital marketing

Chapter 2. A Digital World

1. An _____ is the manufacturing of a good or service within a category. Although _____ is a broad term for any kind of economic production, in economics and urban planning _____ is a synonym for the secondary sector, which is a type of economic activity involved in the manufacturing of raw materials into goods and products.

   There are four key industrial economic sectors: the primary sector, largely raw material extraction industries such as mining and farming; the secondary sector, involving refining, construction, and manufacturing; the tertiary sector, which deals with services (such as law and medicine) and distribution of manufactured goods; and the quaternary sector, a relatively new type of knowledge _____ focusing on technological research, design and development such as computer programming, and biochemistry.

   a. AMAX
   b. Industry
   c. ACNielsen
   d. ADTECH

2. A _____ or personal video recorder (PVR) is a device that records video in a digital format to a disk drive or other memory medium within a device. The term includes stand-alone set-top boxes, portable media players (PMP) and software for personal computers which enables video capture and playback to and from disk. Some consumer electronic manufacturers have started to offer televisions with _____ hardware and software built in to the television itself; LG was first to launch one in 2007.
   a. Power III
   b. 6-3-5 Brainwriting
   c. 180SearchAssistant
   d. Digital video recorder

3. _____ is the practice of promoting products and services using digital distribution channels to reach consumers in a timely, relevant, personal and cost-effective manner.

   Whilst _____ does include many of the techniques and practices contained within the category of Internet Marketing, it extends beyond this by including other channels with which to reach people that do not require the use of The Internet. As a result of this non-reliance on the Internet, the field of _____ includes a whole host of elements such as mobile phones, sms/mms, display / banner ads and digital outdoor.

   a. Relationship marketing
   b. Global marketing
   c. Diversity marketing
   d. Digital marketing

4. _____ is defined by the American _____ Association as the activity, set of institutions, and processes for creating, communicating, delivering, and exchanging offerings that have value for customers, clients, partners, and society at large. The term developed from the original meaning which referred literally to going to market, as in shopping, or going to a market to sell goods or services.

_____ practice tends to be seen as a creative industry, which includes advertising, distribution and selling.

a. Marketing myopia
b. Customer acquisition management
c. Product naming
d. Marketing

5. _____, also referred to as i-marketing, web marketing, online marketing is the marketing of products or services over the Internet.

The Internet has brought many unique benefits to marketing, one of which being lower costs for the distribution of information and media to a global audience. The interactive nature of _____, both in terms of providing instant response and eliciting responses, is a unique quality of the medium.

a. Internet marketing
b. AMAX
c. ACNielsen
d. ADTECH

6. _____ is a form of Internet marketing that seeks to promote websites by increasing their visibility in search engine result pages (SERPs.) According to the _____ Professional Organization, _____ methods include: search engine optimization (or SEO), paid placement, contextual advertising, and paid inclusion. Other sources, including the New York Times, define _____ as the practice of buying paid search listings.

a. Pay for placement
b. Display advertising
c. Search engine marketing
d. Blog marketing

7. In economics, business, retail, and accounting, a _____ is the value of money that has been used up to produce something, and hence is not available for use anymore. In economics, a _____ is an alternative that is given up as a result of a decision. In business, the _____ may be one of acquisition, in which case the amount of money expended to acquire it is counted as _____.

a. Transaction cost
b. Fixed costs
c. Variable cost
d. Cost

8. _____ is the provision of service to customers before, during and after a purchase.

According to Turban et al., '_____ is a series of activities designed to enhance the level of customer satisfaction - that is, the feeling that a product or service has met the customer expectation.'

Its importance varies by product, industry and customer.

a. COPC Inc.
b. Customer experience
c. Facing
d. Customer service

9. _____ is an advertisement in which a particular product specifically mentions a competitor by name for the express purpose of showing why the competitor is inferior to the product naming it.

This should not be confused with parody advertisements, where a fictional product is being advertised for the purpose of poking fun at the particular advertisement, nor should it be confused with the use of a coined brand name for the purpose of comparing the product without actually naming an actual competitor. ('Wikipedia tastes better and is less filling than the Encyclopedia Galactica.')

In the 1980s, during what has been referred to as the cola wars, soft-drink manufacturer Pepsi ran a series of advertisements where people, caught on hidden camera, in a blind taste test, chose Pepsi over rival Coca-Cola.

a. GL-70
b. Cost per conversion
c. Heavy-up
d. Comparative advertising

10. _____ is a broad label that refers to any individuals or households that use goods and services generated within the economy. The concept of a _____ is used in different contexts, so that the usage and significance of the term may vary.

A _____ is a person who uses any product or service.

a. 6-3-5 Brainwriting
b. Consumer
c. 180SearchAssistant
d. Power III

11. _____ or consumer demand or consumption is also known as personal consumption expenditure. It is the largest part of aggregate demand or effective demand at the macroeconomic level. There are two variants of consumption in the aggregate demand model, including induced consumption and autonomous consumption.
   a. Deregulation
   b. Power III
   c. Value added
   d. Consumer spending

12. In economics, _____ is the desire to own something and the ability to pay for it. The term _____ signifies the ability or the willingness to buy a particular commodity at a given point of time .

   a. Demand
   b. Market system
   c. Market dominance
   d. Discretionary spending

13. _____ is the conveying of events in words, images, and sounds often by improvisation or embellishment. Stories or narratives have been shared in every culture and in every land as a means of entertainment, education, preservation of culture and in order to instill moral values. Crucial elements of stories and _____ include plot and characters, as well as the narrative point of view.
   a. Storytelling
   b. 180SearchAssistant
   c. Power III
   d. 6-3-5 Brainwriting

14. A _____ is a structured collection of records or data that is stored in a computer system. The structure is achieved by organizing the data according to a _____ model. The model in most common use today is the relational model.

a. Power III
b. 180SearchAssistant
c. Database
d. 6-3-5 Brainwriting

15. _____ is a form of communication that typically attempts to persuade potential customers to purchase or to consume more of a particular brand of product or service. 'While now central to the contemporary global economy and the reproduction of global production networks, it is only quite recently that _____ has been more than a marginal influence on patterns of sales and production. The formation of modern _____ was intimately bound up with the emergence of new forms of monopoly capitalism around the end of the 19th and beginning of the 20th century as one element in corporate strategies to create, organize and where possible control markets, especially for mass produced consumer goods.
a. ACNielsen
b. ADTECH
c. Advertising
d. AMAX

16. _____ is a form of promotion that uses the Internet and World Wide Web for the expressed purpose of delivering marketing messages to attract customers. Examples of _____ include contextual ads on search engine results pages, banner ads, Rich Media Ads, Social network advertising, online classified advertising, advertising networks and e-mail marketing, including e-mail spam.

Online video directories for brands are a good example of interactive advertising.

a. AMAX
b. ADTECH
c. ACNielsen
d. Online advertising

Chapter 3. Networks

1. _____ is the assignment of objects into groups (called clusters) so that objects from the same cluster are more similar to each other than objects from different clusters. Often similarity is assessed according to a distance measure. _____ is a common technique for statistical data analysis, which is used in many fields, including machine learning, data mining, pattern recognition, image analysis and bioinformatics.
   a. Developed country
   b. Just-In-Case
   c. Clustering
   d. Comparison-Shopping agent

2. _____ is the examining of goods or services from retailers with the intent to purchase at that time. _____ is an activity of selection and/or purchase. In some contexts it is considered a leisure activity as well as an economic one.
   a. Hawkers
   b. Khodebshchik
   c. Discount store
   d. Shopping

3. The _____ is a very large set of interlinked hypertext documents accessed via the Internet. With a Web browser, one can view Web pages that may contain text, images, videos, and other multimedia and navigate between them using hyperlinks. Using concepts from earlier hypertext systems, the _____ was begun in 1992 by the English physicist Sir Tim Berners-Lee, now the Director of the _____ Consortium, and Robert Cailliau, a Belgian computer scientist, while both were working at CERN in Geneva, Switzerland.
   a. 180SearchAssistant
   b. 6-3-5 Brainwriting
   c. Power III
   d. World Wide Web

4. _____ is a form of communication that typically attempts to persuade potential customers to purchase or to consume more of a particular brand of product or service. 'While now central to the contemporary global economy and the reproduction of global production networks, it is only quite recently that _____ has been more than a marginal influence on patterns of sales and production. The formation of modern _____ was intimately bound up with the emergence of new forms of monopoly capitalism around the end of the 19th and beginning of the 20th century as one element in corporate strategies to create, organize and where possible control markets, especially for mass produced consumer goods.
   a. ACNielsen
   b. ADTECH
   c. AMAX
   d. Advertising

Chapter 3. Networks

5. _____ is the process of improving the volume and quality of traffic to a web site from search engines via 'natural' ('organic' or 'algorithmic') search results. Typically, the earlier a site appears in the search results list, the more visitors it will receive from the search engine. _____ may target different kinds of search, including image search, local search, and industry-specific vertical search engines.
   a. 180SearchAssistant
   b. Power III
   c. 6-3-5 Brainwriting
   d. Search engine optimization

6. In economics, an externality or spillover of an economic transaction is an impact on a party that is not directly involved in the transaction. In such a case, prices do not reflect the full costs or benefits in production or consumption of a product or service. A positive impact is called an _____ benefit, while a negative impact is called an _____ cost.
   a. ADTECH
   b. ACNielsen
   c. AMAX
   d. External

7. A _____ is a type of website, usually maintained by an individual with regular entries of commentary, descriptions of events, or other material such as graphics or video. Entries are commonly displayed in reverse-chronological order. '_____' can also be used as a verb, meaning to maintain or add content to a _____.
   a. 6-3-5 Brainwriting
   b. 180SearchAssistant
   c. Power III
   d. Blog

8. _____ is the ability of an individual or group to seclude themselves or information about themselves and thereby reveal themselves selectively. The boundaries and content of what is considered private differ among cultures and individuals, but share basic common themes. _____ is sometimes related to anonymity, the wish to remain unnoticed or unidentified in the public realm.
   a. 6-3-5 Brainwriting
   b. Power III
   c. 180SearchAssistant
   d. Privacy

9. _____ are used for a variety of social and professional groups interacting via the Internet. It does not necessarily mean that there is a strong bond among the members, although Howard Rheingold, author of the book of the same name, mentions that _____ form 'when people carry on public discussions long enough, with sufficient human feeling, to form webs of personal relationships'. An email distribution list may have hundreds of members and the communication which takes place may be merely informational (questions and answers are posted), but members may remain relative strangers and the membership turnover rate could be high.
   a. Power III
   b. 180SearchAssistant
   c. 6-3-5 Brainwriting
   d. Virtual communities

10. A personal and cultural _____ is a relative ethic _____, an assumption upon which implementation can be extrapolated. A _____ system is a set of consistent _____s and measures that is soo not true. A principle _____ is a foundation upon which other _____s and measures of integrity are based.
   a. Package-on-Package
   b. Perceptual maps
   c. Supreme Court of the United States
   d. Value

11. The term _____ refers to several methods by which individuals can avoid receiving unsolicited product or service information. This ability is usually associated with direct marketing campaigns such as telemarketing, e-mail marketing, or direct mail.

The U.S. Federal Government created the National Do Not Call Registry to reduce the telemarketing calls consumers receive at home.

   a. Opt-out
   b. ACNielsen
   c. AMAX
   d. ADTECH

12. _____. People may not recognize the value in offered personalization, such as when firms offer to customize product offers. Many people don't want to receive any such offers, period.
   a. Category Development Index
   b. Bottling lines
   c. Push
   d. Little value placed on potential benefits

Chapter 3. Networks

13. In finance, an _____ is a contract between a buyer and a seller that gives the buyer the right--but not the obligation-- to buy or to sell a particular asset (the underlying asset) at a later day at an agreed price. In return for granting the _____, the seller collects a payment (the premium) from the buyer. A call _____ gives the buyer the right to buy the underlying asset; a put _____ gives the buyer of the _____ the right to sell the underlying asset.
   a. AMAX
   b. ACNielsen
   c. ADTECH
   d. Option

14. _____, also referred to as i-marketing, web marketing, online marketing is the marketing of products or services over the Internet.

    The Internet has brought many unique benefits to marketing, one of which being lower costs for the distribution of information and media to a global audience. The interactive nature of _____, both in terms of providing instant response and eliciting responses, is a unique quality of the medium.

    a. ADTECH
    b. ACNielsen
    c. Internet marketing
    d. AMAX

15. _____ is a form of Internet marketing that seeks to promote websites by increasing their visibility in search engine result pages (SERPs.) According to the _____ Professional Organization, _____ methods include: search engine optimization (or SEO), paid placement, contextual advertising, and paid inclusion. Other sources, including the New York Times, define _____ as the practice of buying paid search listings.
    a. Pay for placement
    b. Display advertising
    c. Blog marketing
    d. Search engine marketing

16. _____ is defined by the American _____ Association as the activity, set of institutions, and processes for creating, communicating, delivering, and exchanging offerings that have value for customers, clients, partners, and society at large. The term developed from the original meaning which referred literally to going to market, as in shopping, or going to a market to sell goods or services.

    _____ practice tends to be seen as a creative industry, which includes advertising, distribution and selling.

a. Product naming
b. Marketing
c. Customer acquisition management
d. Marketing myopia

17. _____ describes the situation when output from (or information about the result of) an event or phenomenon in the past will influence the same event/phenomenon in the present or future. When an event is part of a chain of cause-and-effect that forms a circuit or loop, then the event is said to 'feed back' into itself.

_____ is also a synonym for:

- _____ Signal; the information about the initial event that is the basis for subsequent modification of the event.
- _____ Loop; the causal path that leads from the initial generation of the _____ signal to the subsequent modification of the event.

_____ is a mechanism, process or signal that is looped back to control a system within itself. Such a loop is called a _____ loop.

a. 180SearchAssistant
b. Power III
c. 6-3-5 Brainwriting
d. Feedback

18. _____ is a broad label that refers to any individuals or households that use goods and services generated within the economy. The concept of a _____ is used in different contexts, so that the usage and significance of the term may vary.

A _____ is a person who uses any product or service.

a. Power III
b. Consumer
c. 6-3-5 Brainwriting
d. 180SearchAssistant

19. _____ is the deliberate attempt to manage the public's perception of a subject. The subjects of _____ include people (for example, politicians and performing artists), goods and services, organizations of all kinds, and works of art or entertainment.

Chapter 3. Networks

From a marketing perspective, _____ is one component of promotion.

 a. Little value placed on potential benefits
 b. Brando
 c. Pearson's chi-square
 d. Publicity

20. Human beings are also considered to be _____ because they have the ability to change raw materials into valuable _____. The term Human _____ can also be defined as the skills, energies, talents, abilities and knowledge that are used for the production of goods or the rendering of services. While taking into account human beings as _____, the following things have to be kept in mind:

 - The size of the population
 - The capabilities of the individuals in that population

Many _____ cannot be consumed in their original form. They have to be processed in order to change them into more usable commodities.

 a. Resources
 b. 6-3-5 Brainwriting
 c. 180SearchAssistant
 d. Power III

21. _____ is subcontracting a process, such as product design or manufacturing, to a third-party company. The decision to outsource is often made in the interest of lowering cost or making better use of time and energy costs, redirecting or conserving energy directed at the competencies of a particular business, or to make more efficient use of land, labor, capital, (information) technology and resources. _____ became part of the business lexicon during the 1980s.
 a. In-house
 b. Outsourcing
 c. ACNielsen
 d. Intangible assets

22. _____ is one of the four elements of marketing mix. An organization or set of organizations (go-betweens) involved in the process of making a product or service available for use or consumption by a consumer or business user.

The other three parts of the marketing mix are product, pricing, and promotion.

a. Japan Advertising Photographers' Association
b. Comparison-Shopping agent
c. Distribution
d. Better Living Through Chemistry

Chapter 4. Individuals Online

1. _____, also referred to as i-marketing, web marketing, online marketing is the marketing of products or services over the Internet.

The Internet has brought many unique benefits to marketing, one of which being lower costs for the distribution of information and media to a global audience. The interactive nature of _____, both in terms of providing instant response and eliciting responses, is a unique quality of the medium.

   a. ACNielsen
   b. AMAX
   c. ADTECH
   d. Internet marketing

2. Radio-frequency identification (_____) is the use of an object (typically referred to as an _____ tag) applied to or incorporated into a product, animal, or person for the purpose of identification and tracking using radio waves. Some tags can be read from several meters away and beyond the line of sight of the reader.

Most _____ tags contain at least two parts.

   a. 6-3-5 Brainwriting
   b. RFID
   c. Power III
   d. 180SearchAssistant

3. _____ is defined by the American _____ Association as the activity, set of institutions, and processes for creating, communicating, delivering, and exchanging offerings that have value for customers, clients, partners, and society at large. The term developed from the original meaning which referred literally to going to market, as in shopping, or going to a market to sell goods or services.

_____ practice tends to be seen as a creative industry, which includes advertising, distribution and selling.

   a. Customer acquisition management
   b. Marketing myopia
   c. Product naming
   d. Marketing

4. _____. People may not recognize the value in offered personalization, such as when firms offer to customize product offers. Many people don't want to receive any such offers, period.

a. Push
b. Category Development Index
c. Bottling lines
d. Little value placed on potential benefits

5. On an intranet or B2E Enterprise Web portals, personalization is often based on user attributes such as department, functional area, or role. The term _____ in this context refers to the ability of users to modify the page layout or specify what content should be displayed.

There are two categories of personalizations:

1. Rule-based
2. Content-based

Web personalization models include rules-based filtering, based on 'if this, then that' rules processing, and collaborative filtering, which serves relevant material to customers by combining their own personal preferences with the preferences of like-minded others. Collaborative filtering works well for books, music, video, etc.

a. Customization
b. Movin'
c. Self branding
d. Cashmere Agency

6. _____ or personalisation is tailoring a consumer product, electronic or written medium to a user based on personal details or characteristics they provide. More recently, it has especially been applied in the context of the World Wide Web.

Web pages are personalized based on the interests of an individual.

a. Complex sale
b. Sexism,
c. Flighting
d. Personalization

7. In statistics, an _____ is a term in a statistical model added when the effect of two or more variables is not simply additive. Such a term reflects that the effect of one variable depends on the values of one or more other variables.

Thus, for a response Y and two variables x_1 and x_2 an additive model would be:

$$Y = ax_1 + bx_2 + \text{error}$$

In contrast to this,

$$Y = ax_1 + bx_2 + c(x_1 \times x_2) + \text{error},$$

is an example of a model with an _____ between variables x_1 and x_2 ('error' refers to the random variable whose value by which y differs from the expected value of y.)

   a. AMAX
   b. Interaction
   c. ACNielsen
   d. ADTECH

8. _____ is anything that is generally accepted as payment for goods and services and repayment of debts. The main uses of _____ are as a medium of exchange, a unit of account, and a store of value. Some authors explicitly require _____ to be a standard of deferred payment.
   a. Money
   b. Leading indicator
   c. Law of supply
   d. Microeconomics

9. _____ or _____ data refers to selected population characteristics as used in government, marketing or opinion research, or the _____ profiles used in such research. Note the distinction from the term 'demography' Commonly-used _____ include race, age, income, disabilities, mobility (in terms of travel time to work or number of vehicles available), educational attainment, home ownership, employment status, and even location.
   a. AStore
   b. African Americans
   c. Albert Einstein
   d. Demographic

10. _____ is one of the four elements of marketing mix. An organization or set of organizations (go-betweens) involved in the process of making a product or service available for use or consumption by a consumer or business user.

The other three parts of the marketing mix are product, pricing, and promotion.

a. Comparison-Shopping agent
b. Distribution
c. Japan Advertising Photographers' Association
d. Better Living Through Chemistry

11. _____ is a contract between two parties, one being the employer and the other being the employee. An employee may be defined as: 'A person in the service of another under any contract of hire, express or implied, oral or written, where the employer has the power or right to control and direct the employee in the material details of how the work is to be performed.' Black's Law Dictionary page 471 (5th ed. 1979.)
  a. ADTECH
  b. ACNielsen
  c. Employment
  d. AMAX

12. _____ is a broad label that refers to any individuals or households that use goods and services generated within the economy. The concept of a _____ is used in different contexts, so that the usage and significance of the term may vary.

A _____ is a person who uses any product or service.

  a. Consumer
  b. 180SearchAssistant
  c. 6-3-5 Brainwriting
  d. Power III

13. _____ is the study of when, why, how, where and what people do or do not buy products. It blends elements from psychology, sociology, social psychology, anthropology and economics. It attempts to understand the buyer decision making process, both individually and in groups. It studies characteristics of individual consumers such as demographics and behavioural variables in an attempt to understand people's wants. It also tries to assess influences on the consumer from groups such as family, friends, reference groups, and society in general.
  a. Multidimensional scaling
  b. Communal marketing
  c. Consumer confidence
  d. Consumer behavior

14. _____ is a form of Internet marketing that seeks to promote websites by increasing their visibility in search engine result pages (SERPs.) According to the _____ Professional Organization, _____ methods include: search engine optimization (or SEO), paid placement, contextual advertising, and paid inclusion. Other sources, including the New York Times, define _____ as the practice of buying paid search listings.
   a. Search engine marketing
   b. Blog marketing
   c. Pay for placement
   d. Display advertising

15. _____ is a form of communication that typically attempts to persuade potential customers to purchase or to consume more of a particular brand of product or service. 'While now central to the contemporary global economy and the reproduction of global production networks, it is only quite recently that _____ has been more than a marginal influence on patterns of sales and production. The formation of modern _____ was intimately bound up with the emergence of new forms of monopoly capitalism around the end of the 19th and beginning of the 20th century as one element in corporate strategies to create, organize and where possible control markets, especially for mass produced consumer goods.
   a. ADTECH
   b. AMAX
   c. ACNielsen
   d. Advertising

16. In the mathematical discipline of graph theory a _____ or edge-independent set in a graph is a set of edges without common vertices. It may also be an entire graph consisting of edges without common vertices.

Given a graph G = (V,E), a _____ M in G is a set of pairwise non-adjacent edges; that is, no two edges share a common vertex.

   a. 180SearchAssistant
   b. Power III
   c. Matching
   d. 6-3-5 Brainwriting

17. In psychology, philosophy, and the cognitive sciences, _____ is the process of attaining awareness or understanding of sensory information. It is a task far more complex than was imagined in the 1950s and 1960s, when it was predicted that building perceiving machines would take about a decade, a goal which is still very far from fruition. The word _____ comes from the Latin words _____, percepio, meaning 'receiving, collecting, action of taking possession, apprehension with the mind or senses.'

_____ is one of the oldest fields in psychology.

a. Power III
b. 180SearchAssistant
c. Groupthink
d. Perception

18. The _____ is the de facto national library of the United States and the research arm of the United States Congress. Located in three buildings in Washington, D.C., it is the largest library in the world by shelf space and holds the largest number of books. The head of the Library is the Librarian of Congress, currently James H. Billington.
   a. Power III
   b. 6-3-5 Brainwriting
   c. 180SearchAssistant
   d. Library of Congress

19. In the field of computer security, _____ is the criminally fraudulent process of attempting to acquire sensitive information such as usernames, passwords and credit card details by masquerading as a trustworthy entity in an electronic communication. Communications purporting to be from popular social web sites, auction sites, online payment processors or IT Administrators are commonly used to lure the unsuspecting public. _____ is typically carried out by e-mail or instant messaging, and it often directs users to enter details at a fake website whose look and feel are almost identical to the legitimate one.
   a. Joe job
   b. Directory Harvest Attack
   c. Phishing
   d. Telemarketing

20. The most important feature of a contract is that one party makes an _____ for an arrangement that another accepts. This can be called a 'concurrence of wills' or 'ad idem' (meeting of the minds) of two or more parties. The concept is somewhat contested.
   a. ADTECH
   b. ACNielsen
   c. AMAX
   d. Offer

Chapter 5. Web Business Models

1. A _____ is a framework for creating economic, social, and/or other forms of value. The term _____ is thus used for a broad range of informal and formal descriptions to represent core aspects of a business, including purpose, offerings, strategies, infrastructure, organizational structures, trading practices, and operational processes and policies.

   In the most basic sense, a _____ is the method of doing business by which a company can sustain itself -- that is, generate revenue.

   a. Service provider
   b. Pay to surf
   c. Yield management
   d. Business model

2. In marketing, customer _____, lifetime customer value (LCV), or _____ (LTV) and a new concept of 'customer life cycle management' is the present value of the future cash flows attributed to the customer relationship. Use of customer _____ as a marketing metric tends to place greater emphasis on customer service and long-term customer satisfaction, rather than on maximizing short-term sales.

   Customer _____ has intuitive appeal as a marketing concept, because in theory it represents exactly how much each customer is worth in monetary terms, and therefore exactly how much a marketing department should be willing to spend to acquire each customer.

   a. Lifetime value
   b. Value chain
   c. Brand infiltration
   d. Sweepstakes

3. A personal and cultural _____ is a relative ethic _____, an assumption upon which implementation can be extrapolated. A _____ system is a set of consistent _____s and measures that is soo not true. A principle _____ is a foundation upon which other _____s and measures of integrity are based.
   a. Package-on-Package
   b. Perceptual maps
   c. Supreme Court of the United States
   d. Value

4. _____, also referred to as i-marketing, web marketing, online marketing is the marketing of products or services over the Internet.

   The Internet has brought many unique benefits to marketing, one of which being lower costs for the distribution of information and media to a global audience. The interactive nature of _____, both in terms of providing instant response and eliciting responses, is a unique quality of the medium.

a. AMAX
b. ACNielsen
c. ADTECH
d. Internet marketing

5. _____ is defined by the American _____ Association as the activity, set of institutions, and processes for creating, communicating, delivering, and exchanging offerings that have value for customers, clients, partners, and society at large. The term developed from the original meaning which referred literally to going to market, as in shopping, or going to a market to sell goods or services.

_____ practice tends to be seen as a creative industry, which includes advertising, distribution and selling.

a. Product naming
b. Customer acquisition management
c. Marketing myopia
d. Marketing

6. _____ is a form of Internet marketing that seeks to promote websites by increasing their visibility in search engine result pages (SERPs.) According to the _____ Professional Organization, _____ methods include: search engine optimization (or SEO), paid placement, contextual advertising, and paid inclusion. Other sources, including the New York Times, define _____ as the practice of buying paid search listings.

a. Display advertising
b. Blog marketing
c. Pay for placement
d. Search engine marketing

7. _____ is one of the four elements of marketing mix. An organization or set of organizations (go-betweens) involved in the process of making a product or service available for use or consumption by a consumer or business user.

The other three parts of the marketing mix are product, pricing, and promotion.

a. Japan Advertising Photographers' Association
b. Better Living Through Chemistry
c. Comparison-Shopping agent
d. Distribution

8. In statistics, an _____ is a term in a statistical model added when the effect of two or more variables is not simply additive. Such a term reflects that the effect of one variable depends on the values of one or more other variables.

Thus, for a response Y and two variables x_1 and x_2 an additive model would be:

$$Y = ax_1 + bx_2 + \text{error}$$

In contrast to this,

$$Y = ax_1 + bx_2 + c(x_1 \times x_2) + \text{error},$$

is an example of a model with an _____ between variables x_1 and x_2 ('error' refers to the random variable whose value by which y differs from the expected value of y.)

a. ACNielsen
b. AMAX
c. Interaction
d. ADTECH

9. _____ refers to any advertising that is linked to specific words or phrases. Common forms of _____ are known by many other terms including pay per click (PPC) and cost per action (CPA.) There are multiple variations each starting with 'pay per' or 'cost per' such as pay per action (PPA), pay per cost (PPC), cost per mille (CPM.)

a. Hover ads
b. Search advertising
c. Semantic targeting
d. Keyword advertising

10. _____ is a form of communication that typically attempts to persuade potential customers to purchase or to consume more of a particular brand of product or service. 'While now central to the contemporary global economy and the reproduction of global production networks, it is only quite recently that _____ has been more than a marginal influence on patterns of sales and production. The formation of modern _____ was intimately bound up with the emergence of new forms of monopoly capitalism around the end of the 19th and beginning of the 20th century as one element in corporate strategies to create, organize and where possible control markets, especially for mass produced consumer goods.

a. ACNielsen
b. AMAX
c. ADTECH
d. Advertising

11. _____,, is a common tool in the retail industry to create the look of a perfectly stocked store by pulling all of the products on a display or shelf to the front, as well as downstacking all the canned and stacked items. It is also done to keep the store appearing neat and organized.

The workers who face commonly have jobs doing other things in the store such as customer service, stocking shelves, daytime cleaning, bagging and carryouts, etc.

a. Foviance
b. Facing
c. Customer Experience Analytics
d. Customer Integrated System

12. _____ is an advertisement in which a particular product specifically mentions a competitor by name for the express purpose of showing why the competitor is inferior to the product naming it.

This should not be confused with parody advertisements, where a fictional product is being advertised for the purpose of poking fun at the particular advertisement, nor should it be confused with the use of a coined brand name for the purpose of comparing the product without actually naming an actual competitor. ('Wikipedia tastes better and is less filling than the Encyclopedia Galactica.')

In the 1980s, during what has been referred to as the cola wars, soft-drink manufacturer Pepsi ran a series of advertisements where people, caught on hidden camera, in a blind taste test, chose Pepsi over rival Coca-Cola.

a. Heavy-up
b. GL-70
c. Cost per conversion
d. Comparative advertising

13. _____ consists of the sale of goods or merchandise from a fixed location, such as a department store or kiosk in small or individual lots for direct consumption by the purchaser. _____ may include subordinated services, such as delivery. Purchasers may be individuals or businesses.

a. Retailing
b. Charity shop
c. Warehouse store
d. Thrifting

14. _____ is a form of promotion that uses the Internet and World Wide Web for the expressed purpose of delivering marketing messages to attract customers. Examples of _____ include contextual ads on search engine results pages, banner ads, Rich Media Ads, Social network advertising, online classified advertising, advertising networks and e-mail marketing, including e-mail spam.

Online video directories for brands are a good example of interactive advertising.

a. Online advertising
b. ADTECH
c. ACNielsen
d. AMAX

15. In economics, business, retail, and accounting, a _____ is the value of money that has been used up to produce something, and hence is not available for use anymore. In economics, a _____ is an alternative that is given up as a result of a decision. In business, the _____ may be one of acquisition, in which case the amount of money expended to acquire it is counted as _____.
   a. Cost
   b. Transaction cost
   c. Variable cost
   d. Fixed costs

16. _____ is the provision of service to customers before, during and after a purchase.

According to Turban et al., '_____ is a series of activities designed to enhance the level of customer satisfaction - that is, the feeling that a product or service has met the customer expectation.'

Its importance varies by product, industry and customer.

   a. Customer experience
   b. COPC Inc.
   c. Facing
   d. Customer service

17. A _____ or logistics network is the system of organizations, people, technology, activities, information and resources involved in moving a product or service from supplier to customer. _____ activities transform natural resources, raw materials and components into a finished product that is delivered to the end customer. In sophisticated _____ systems, used products may re-enter the _____ at any point where residual value is recyclable.
   a. Supply chain network
   b. Purchasing
   c. Demand chain management
   d. Supply chain

18. A _____ is a collection of symbols, experiences and associations connected with a product, a service, a person or any other artifact or entity.

Chapter 5. Web Business Models

_____s have become increasingly important components of culture and the economy, now being described as 'cultural accessories and personal philosophies'.

Some people distinguish the psychological aspect of a _____ from the experiential aspect.

   a. Brand equity
   b. Brand
   c. Brandable software
   d. Store brand

19. Quality management can be considered to have three main components: quality control, quality assurance and _____. Quality management is focused not only on product quality, but also the means to achieve it. Quality management therefore uses quality assurance and control of processes as well as products to achieve more consistent quality.
   a. 6-3-5 Brainwriting
   b. Power III
   c. Quality improvement
   d. 180SearchAssistant

20. _____ is an Internet-based marketing practice in which a business rewards one or more affiliates for each visitor or customer brought about by the affiliate's marketing efforts.

_____ is also the name of the industry where a number of different types of companies and individuals are performing this form of Internet marketing, including affiliate networks, affiliate management companies, and in-house affiliate managers, specialized third party vendors, and various types of affiliates/publishers who promote the products and services of their partners.

_____ overlaps with other Internet marketing methods to some degree, because affiliates often use regular advertising methods.

   a. ADTECH
   b. ACNielsen
   c. AMAX
   d. Affiliate marketing

21. A _____ is the price one pays as remuneration for services, especially the honorarium paid to a doctor, lawyer, consultant, or other member of a learned profession. _____s usually allow for overhead, wages, costs, and markup.

Traditionally, professionals in Great Britain received a _____ in contradistinction to a payment, salary, or wage, and would often use guineas rather than pounds as units of account.

a. Fee
b. Transfer pricing
c. Price shading
d. Price war

22. _____ is one of the four Ps of the marketing mix. The other three aspects are product, promotion, and place. It is also a key variable in microeconomic price allocation theory.

a. Pricing
b. Competitor indexing
c. Price
d. Relationship based pricing

23. An _____ is the manufacturing of a good or service within a category. Although _____ is a broad term for any kind of economic production, in economics and urban planning _____ is a synonym for the secondary sector, which is a type of economic activity involved in the manufacturing of raw materials into goods and products.

There are four key industrial economic sectors: the primary sector, largely raw material extraction industries such as mining and farming; the secondary sector, involving refining, construction, and manufacturing; the tertiary sector, which deals with services (such as law and medicine) and distribution of manufactured goods; and the quaternary sector, a relatively new type of knowledge _____ focusing on technological research, design and development such as computer programming, and biochemistry.

a. AMAX
b. ADTECH
c. Industry
d. ACNielsen

Chapter 6. Online Branding

1. A _____ or personal video recorder (PVR) is a device that records video in a digital format to a disk drive or other memory medium within a device. The term includes stand-alone set-top boxes, portable media players (PMP) and software for personal computers which enables video capture and playback to and from disk. Some consumer electronic manufacturers have started to offer televisions with _____ hardware and software built in to the television itself; LG was first to launch one in 2007.
   a. 6-3-5 Brainwriting
   b. 180SearchAssistant
   c. Digital video recorder
   d. Power III

2. _____ refers to any advertising that is linked to specific words or phrases. Common forms of _____ are known by many other terms including pay per click (PPC) and cost per action (CPA.) There are multiple variations each starting with 'pay per' or 'cost per' such as pay per action (PPA), pay per cost (PPC), cost per mille (CPM.)
   a. Hover ads
   b. Keyword advertising
   c. Semantic targeting
   d. Search advertising

3. _____ is a market coverage strategy in which a firm decides to ignore market segment differences and go after the whole market with one offer.it is type of marketing (or attempting to sell through persuasion) of a product to a wide audience. The idea is to broadcast a message that will reach the largest number of people possible. Traditionally _____ has focused on radio, television and newspapers as the medium used to reach this broad audience.
   a. Cyberdoc
   b. Business-to-consumer
   c. Marketspace
   d. Mass marketing

4. _____ is a term used to denote a section of the media specifically designed to reach a very large audience such as the population of a nation state. It was coined in the 1920s with the advent of nationwide radio networks, mass-circulation newspapers and magazines, although _____ were present centuries before the term became common. The term public media has a similar meaning: it is the sum of the public mass distributors of news and entertainment across media such as newspapers, television, radio, broadcasting, which may require union membership in some large markets such as Newspaper Guild, AFTRA, ' text publishers.
   a. 6-3-5 Brainwriting
   b. 180SearchAssistant
   c. Mass media
   d. Power III

Chapter 6. Online Branding 37

5. _____ is a form of Internet marketing that seeks to promote websites by increasing their visibility in search engine result pages (SERPs.) According to the _____ Professional Organization, _____ methods include: search engine optimization (or SEO), paid placement, contextual advertising, and paid inclusion. Other sources, including the New York Times, define _____ as the practice of buying paid search listings.
   a. Search engine marketing
   b. Blog marketing
   c. Pay for placement
   d. Display advertising

6. _____ is a form of communication that typically attempts to persuade potential customers to purchase or to consume more of a particular brand of product or service. 'While now central to the contemporary global economy and the reproduction of global production networks, it is only quite recently that _____ has been more than a marginal influence on patterns of sales and production. The formation of modern _____ was intimately bound up with the emergence of new forms of monopoly capitalism around the end of the 19th and beginning of the 20th century as one element in corporate strategies to create, organize and where possible control markets, especially for mass produced consumer goods.
   a. ADTECH
   b. ACNielsen
   c. AMAX
   d. Advertising

7. _____,, is a common tool in the retail industry to create the look of a perfectly stocked store by pulling all of the products on a display or shelf to the front, as well as downstacking all the canned and stacked items. It is also done to keep the store appearing neat and organized.

The workers who face commonly have jobs doing other things in the store such as customer service, stocking shelves, daytime cleaning, bagging and carryouts, etc.

   a. Foviance
   b. Customer Integrated System
   c. Customer Experience Analytics
   d. Facing

8. _____ is defined by the American _____ Association as the activity, set of institutions, and processes for creating, communicating, delivering, and exchanging offerings that have value for customers, clients, partners, and society at large. The term developed from the original meaning which referred literally to going to market, as in shopping, or going to a market to sell goods or services.

_____ practice tends to be seen as a creative industry, which includes advertising, distribution and selling.

a. Product naming
b. Marketing myopia
c. Marketing
d. Customer acquisition management

9. _____ is one of the four elements of marketing mix. An organization or set of organizations (go-betweens) involved in the process of making a product or service available for use or consumption by a consumer or business user.

The other three parts of the marketing mix are product, pricing, and promotion.

a. Better Living Through Chemistry
b. Comparison-Shopping agent
c. Distribution
d. Japan Advertising Photographers' Association

10. A _____ is a collection of symbols, experiences and associations connected with a product, a service, a person or any other artifact or entity.

_____s have become increasingly important components of culture and the economy, now being described as 'cultural accessories and personal philosophies'.

Some people distinguish the psychological aspect of a _____ from the experiential aspect.

a. Brandable software
b. Brand equity
c. Store brand
d. Brand

11. _____ refers to the marketing effects or outcomes that accrue to a product with its brand name compared with those that would accrue if the same product did not have the brand name . And, at the root of these marketing effects is consumers' knowledge. In other words, consumers' knowledge about a brand makes manufacturers/advertisers respond differently or adopt appropriately adapt measures for the marketing of the brand .
a. Brand aversion
b. Brand image
c. Product extension
d. Brand equity

Chapter 6. Online Branding

12. _____ is an advertisement in which a particular product specifically mentions a competitor by name for the express purpose of showing why the competitor is inferior to the product naming it.

This should not be confused with parody advertisements, where a fictional product is being advertised for the purpose of poking fun at the particular advertisement, nor should it be confused with the use of a coined brand name for the purpose of comparing the product without actually naming an actual competitor. ('Wikipedia tastes better and is less filling than the Encyclopedia Galactica.')

In the 1980s, during what has been referred to as the cola wars, soft-drink manufacturer Pepsi ran a series of advertisements where people, caught on hidden camera, in a blind taste test, chose Pepsi over rival Coca-Cola.

a. Cost per conversion
b. Heavy-up
c. Comparative advertising
d. GL-70

13. A personal and cultural _____ is a relative ethic _____, an assumption upon which implementation can be extrapolated. A _____ system is a set of consistent _____s and measures that is soo not true. A principle _____ is a foundation upon which other _____s and measures of integrity are based.

a. Perceptual maps
b. Value
c. Supreme Court of the United States
d. Package-on-Package

14. _____ is subcontracting a process, such as product design or manufacturing, to a third-party company. The decision to outsource is often made in the interest of lowering cost or making better use of time and energy costs, redirecting or conserving energy directed at the competencies of a particular business, or to make more efficient use of land, labor, capital, (information) technology and resources. _____ became part of the business lexicon during the 1980s.

a. Outsourcing
b. Intangible assets
c. ACNielsen
d. In-house

15. _____ often refers to either primary or secondary research. Secondary research involves a company using information compiled from various sources, which is about a new or existing product. The advantages of secondary research are that it is relatively cheap and easily accessible.

a. Questionnaire
b. Mystery shoppers
c. Mystery shopping
d. Market research

16. A _____ is a plan of action designed to achieve a particular goal.

_____ is different from tactics. In military terms, tactics is concerned with the conduct of an engagement while _____ is concerned with how different engagements are linked.

a. Strategy
b. Power III
c. 6-3-5 Brainwriting
d. 180SearchAssistant

17. _____ is an Internet-based marketing practice in which a business rewards one or more affiliates for each visitor or customer brought about by the affiliate's marketing efforts.

_____ is also the name of the industry where a number of different types of companies and individuals are performing this form of Internet marketing, including affiliate networks, affiliate management companies, and in-house affiliate managers, specialized third party vendors, and various types of affiliates/publishers who promote the products and services of their partners.

_____ overlaps with other Internet marketing methods to some degree, because affiliates often use regular advertising methods.

a. ACNielsen
b. AMAX
c. Affiliate marketing
d. ADTECH

18. A _____ is typically the attributes one associates with a brand, how the brand owner wants the consumer to perceive the brand - and by extension the branded company, organization, product or service. The brand owner will seek to bridge the gap between the _____ and the brand identity.

a. Status brand
b. Brand loyalty
c. Brand equity
d. Brand image

19. _____ is the structure of brands within an organizational entity. It is the way in which the brands within a company's portfolio are related to, and differentiated from, one another. The architecture should define the different leagues of branding within the organization; how the corporate brand and sub-brands relate to and support each other; and how the sub-brands reflect or reinforce the core purpose of the corporate brand to which they belong.

a. Channel conflict
b. Status brand
c. Brand architecture
d. Corporate colours

20. A _____ is a process that can allow an organization to concentrate its limited resources on the greatest opportunities to increase sales and achieve a sustainable competitive advantage. A _____ should be centered around the key concept that customer satisfaction is the main goal.

A _____ is most effective when it is an integral component of corporate strategy, defining how the organization will successfully engage customers, prospects, and competitors in the market arena.

a. Marketing strategy
b. Societal marketing
c. Psychographic
d. Cyberdoc

21. The phrase _____ refers to the aspect of corporate strategy, corporate finance and management dealing with the buying, selling and combining of different companies that can aid, finance, or help a growing company in a given industry grow rapidly without having to create another business entity.

An acquisition, also known as a takeover or a buyout, is the buying of one company (the 'target') by another. An acquisition may be friendly or hostile.

a. Mergers and acquisitions
b. 180SearchAssistant
c. Power III
d. 6-3-5 Brainwriting

22. _____, according to The American Marketing Association, is 'a planning process designed to assure that all brand contacts received by a customer or prospect for a product, service, or organization are relevant to that person and consistent over time.' (Marketing Power Dictionary)

_____ is a term used to describe a holistic approach to marketing. It aims to ensure consistency of message and the complementary use of media. The concept includes online and offline marketing channels.

   a. ACNielsen
   b. AMAX
   c. ADTECH
   d. Integrated marketing communications

23. _____ refers to messages and related media used to communicate with a market. Those who practice advertising, branding, direct marketing, graphic design, marketing, packaging, promotion, publicity, sponsorship, public relations, sales, sales promotion and online marketing are termed marketing communicators, _____ managers, or more briefly as marcom managers.
   a. Marketing communication
   b. Merchandising
   c. Merchandise
   d. Sales promotion

24. _____. People may not recognize the value in offered personalization, such as when firms offer to customize product offers. Many people don't want to receive any such offers, period.
   a. Category Development Index
   b. Little value placed on potential benefits
   c. Bottling lines
   d. Push

25. _____, in marketing, consists of a consumer's commitment to repurchase the brand and can be demonstrated by repeated buying of a product or service or other positive behaviors such as word of mouth advocacy. True _____ implies that the consumer is willing, at least on occasion, to put aside their own desires in the interest of the brand. _____ has been proclaimed by some to be the ultimate goal of marketing.
   a. Brand implementation
   b. Brand loyalty
   c. Brand awareness
   d. Trade Symbols

26. A _____ is a community formed on the basis of attachment to a product or marque. Recent developments in marketing and in research in consumer behavior result in stressing the connection between brand, individual identity and culture. Among the concepts developed to explain the behavior of consumers, the concept of a _____ focuses on the connections between consumers.
   a. Customer Integrated System
   b. Customer intimacy
   c. Foviance
   d. Brand community

Chapter 7. Usability, Credibility, and Persuasion

1. A _____ is a collection of symbols, experiences and associations connected with a product, a service, a person or any other artifact or entity.

   _____s have become increasingly important components of culture and the economy, now being described as 'cultural accessories and personal philosophies'.

   Some people distinguish the psychological aspect of a _____ from the experiential aspect.

   a. Brand
   b. Store brand
   c. Brandable software
   d. Brand equity

2. _____ is the structure of brands within an organizational entity. It is the way in which the brands within a company's portfolio are related to, and differentiated from, one another. The architecture should define the different leagues of branding within the organization; how the corporate brand and sub-brands relate to and support each other; and how the sub-brands reflect or reinforce the core purpose of the corporate brand to which they belong.
   a. Status brand
   b. Corporate colours
   c. Brand architecture
   d. Channel conflict

3. _____ is a form of communication that typically attempts to persuade potential customers to purchase or to consume more of a particular brand of product or service. 'While now central to the contemporary global economy and the reproduction of global production networks, it is only quite recently that _____ has been more than a marginal influence on patterns of sales and production. The formation of modern _____ was intimately bound up with the emergence of new forms of monopoly capitalism around the end of the 19th and beginning of the 20th century as one element in corporate strategies to create, organize and where possible control markets, especially for mass produced consumer goods.
   a. AMAX
   b. ADTECH
   c. ACNielsen
   d. Advertising

4. In the mathematical discipline of graph theory a _____ or edge-independent set in a graph is a set of edges without common vertices. It may also be an entire graph consisting of edges without common vertices.

   Given a graph G = (V,E), a _____ M in G is a set of pairwise non-adjacent edges; that is, no two edges share a common vertex.

a. Power III
b. 180SearchAssistant
c. 6-3-5 Brainwriting
d. Matching

5. On an intranet or B2E Enterprise Web portals, personalization is often based on user attributes such as department, functional area, or role. The term _____ in this context refers to the ability of users to modify the page layout or specify what content should be displayed.

There are two categories of personalizations:

1. Rule-based
2. Content-based

Web personalization models include rules-based filtering, based on 'if this, then that' rules processing, and collaborative filtering, which serves relevant material to customers by combining their own personal preferences with the preferences of like-minded others. Collaborative filtering works well for books, music, video, etc.

a. Self branding
b. Movin'
c. Cashmere Agency
d. Customization

6. _____ or personalisation is tailoring a consumer product, electronic or written medium to a user based on personal details or characteristics they provide. More recently, it has especially been applied in the context of the World Wide Web.

Web pages are personalized based on the interests of an individual.

a. Complex sale
b. Flighting
c. Personalization
d. Sexism,

Chapter 7. Usability, Credibility, and Persuasion

7. _____ is the process of using quantitative methods and qualitative methods to evaluate consumer response to a product idea prior to the introduction of a product to the market. It can also be used to generate communication designed to alter consumer attitudes toward existing products. These methods involve the evaluation by consumers of product concepts having certain rational benefits, such as 'a detergent that removes stains but is gentle on fabrics,' or non-rational benefits, such as 'a shampoo that lets you be yourself.' Such methods are commonly referred to as _____ and have been performed using field surveys, personal interviews and focus groups, in combination with various quantitative methods, to generate and evaluate product concepts.
   a. Market analysis
   b. Concept testing
   c. Cross tabulation
   d. Logit analysis

8. A personal and cultural _____ is a relative ethic _____, an assumption upon which implementation can be extrapolated. A _____ system is a set of consistent _____s and measures that is soo not true. A principle _____ is a foundation upon which other _____s and measures of integrity are based.
   a. Perceptual maps
   b. Value
   c. Package-on-Package
   d. Supreme Court of the United States

9.

_____ is a systematic method to improve the 'value' of goods or products and services by using an examination of function. Value, as defined, is the ratio of function to cost. Value can therefore be increased by either improving the function or reducing the cost.

   a. Power III
   b. Productivity
   c. 180SearchAssistant
   d. Value engineering

10. In economics, business, retail, and accounting, a _____ is the value of money that has been used up to produce something, and hence is not available for use anymore. In economics, a _____ is an alternative that is given up as a result of a decision. In business, the _____ may be one of acquisition, in which case the amount of money expended to acquire it is counted as _____.

a. Variable cost
b. Transaction cost
c. Cost
d. Fixed costs

11. _____ is one of the four elements of marketing mix. An organization or set of organizations (go-betweens) involved in the process of making a product or service available for use or consumption by a consumer or business user.

The other three parts of the marketing mix are product, pricing, and promotion.

a. Comparison-Shopping agent
b. Distribution
c. Japan Advertising Photographers' Association
d. Better Living Through Chemistry

12. An _____ is the manufacturing of a good or service within a category. Although _____ is a broad term for any kind of economic production, in economics and urban planning _____ is a synonym for the secondary sector, which is a type of economic activity involved in the manufacturing of raw materials into goods and products.

There are four key industrial economic sectors: the primary sector, largely raw material extraction industries such as mining and farming; the secondary sector, involving refining, construction, and manufacturing; the tertiary sector, which deals with services (such as law and medicine) and distribution of manufactured goods; and the quaternary sector, a relatively new type of knowledge _____ focusing on technological research, design and development such as computer programming, and biochemistry.

a. ACNielsen
b. Industry
c. AMAX
d. ADTECH

13. _____ is the suppression of speech or deletion of communicative material which may be considered objectionable, harmful, sensitive, or inconvenient to the government or media organizations as determined by a censor.

The rationale for _____ is different for various types of information censored:

- Moral _____, is the removal of materials that are obscene or otherwise morally questionable. Pornography, for example, is often censored under this rationale, especially child pornography, which is censored in most jurisdictions in the world.
- Military _____ is the process of keeping military intelligence and tactics confidential and away from the enemy. This is used to counter espionage, which is the process of gleaning military information. Very often, militaries will also attempt to suppress politically inconvenient information even if that information has no actual intelligence value.
- Political _____ occurs when governments hold back information from their citizens. The logic is to exert control over the populace and prevent free expression that might foment rebellion.
- Religious _____ is the means by which any material objectionable to a certain faith is removed. This often involves a dominant religion forcing limitations on less prevalent ones. Alternatively, one religion may shun the works of another when they believe the content is not appropriate for their faith.
- Corporate _____ is the process by which editors in corporate media outlets intervene to halt the publishing of information that portrays their business or business partners in a negative light.

Strict _____ existed in the Eastern Bloc. Throughout the bloc, the various ministries of culture held a tight reign on their writers. Cultural products there reflected the propaganda needs of the state.

a. 6-3-5 Brainwriting
b. Power III
c. 180SearchAssistant
d. Censorship

14. _____ is a form of social influence. It is the process of guiding people toward the adoption of an idea, attitude, or action by rational and symbolic (though not always logical) means. It is strategy of problem-solving relying on 'appeals' rather than coercion.
a. Power III
b. 180SearchAssistant
c. 6-3-5 Brainwriting
d. Persuasion

15. _____ is the imitation of some real thing, state of affairs, or process. The act of simulating something generally entails representing certain key characteristics or behaviors of a selected physical or abstract system.

_____ is used in many contexts, including the modeling of natural systems or human systems in order to gain insight into their functioning.

a. Simulation
b. 6-3-5 Brainwriting
c. 180SearchAssistant
d. Power III

Chapter 8. Traffic Building

1. _____ refers to any advertising that is linked to specific words or phrases. Common forms of _____ are known by many other terms including pay per click (PPC) and cost per action (CPA.) There are multiple variations each starting with 'pay per' or 'cost per' such as pay per action (PPA), pay per cost (PPC), cost per mille (CPM.)
    a. Keyword advertising
    b. Semantic targeting
    c. Hover ads
    d. Search advertising

2. _____ is a form of Internet marketing that seeks to promote websites by increasing their visibility in search engine result pages (SERPs.) According to the _____ Professional Organization, _____ methods include: search engine optimization (or SEO), paid placement, contextual advertising, and paid inclusion. Other sources, including the New York Times, define _____ as the practice of buying paid search listings.
    a. Blog marketing
    b. Pay for placement
    c. Display advertising
    d. Search engine marketing

3. _____ is a form of communication that typically attempts to persuade potential customers to purchase or to consume more of a particular brand of product or service. 'While now central to the contemporary global economy and the reproduction of global production networks, it is only quite recently that _____ has been more than a marginal influence on patterns of sales and production. The formation of modern _____ was intimately bound up with the emergence of new forms of monopoly capitalism around the end of the 19th and beginning of the 20th century as one element in corporate strategies to create, organize and where possible control markets, especially for mass produced consumer goods.
    a. Advertising
    b. ACNielsen
    c. ADTECH
    d. AMAX

4. _____ is defined by the American _____ Association as the activity, set of institutions, and processes for creating, communicating, delivering, and exchanging offerings that have value for customers, clients, partners, and society at large. The term developed from the original meaning which referred literally to going to market, as in shopping, or going to a market to sell goods or services.

_____ practice tends to be seen as a creative industry, which includes advertising, distribution and selling.

    a. Customer acquisition management
    b. Product naming
    c. Marketing myopia
    d. Marketing

5. A personal and cultural _____ is a relative ethic _____, an assumption upon which implementation can be extrapolated. A _____ system is a set of consistent _____s and measures that is soo not true. A principle _____ is a foundation upon which other _____s and measures of integrity are based.
   a. Supreme Court of the United States
   b. Value
   c. Package-on-Package
   d. Perceptual maps

6. _____ is the process of improving the volume and quality of traffic to a web site from search engines via 'natural' ('organic' or 'algorithmic') search results. Typically, the earlier a site appears in the search results list, the more visitors it will receive from the search engine. _____ may target different kinds of search, including image search, local search, and industry-specific vertical search engines.
   a. 180SearchAssistant
   b. Power III
   c. 6-3-5 Brainwriting
   d. Search engine optimization

7. In economics, an externality or spillover of an economic transaction is an impact on a party that is not directly involved in the transaction. In such a case, prices do not reflect the full costs or benefits in production or consumption of a product or service. A positive impact is called an _____ benefit, while a negative impact is called an _____ cost.
   a. ADTECH
   b. External
   c. ACNielsen
   d. AMAX

8. A _____ is a collection of symbols, experiences and associations connected with a product, a service, a person or any other artifact or entity.

_____s have become increasingly important components of culture and the economy, now being described as 'cultural accessories and personal philosophies'.

Some people distinguish the psychological aspect of a _____ from the experiential aspect.

   a. Brand
   b. Store brand
   c. Brandable software
   d. Brand equity

9. _____ is the structure of brands within an organizational entity. It is the way in which the brands within a company's portfolio are related to, and differentiated from, one another. The architecture should define the different leagues of branding within the organization; how the corporate brand and sub-brands relate to and support each other; and how the sub-brands reflect or reinforce the core purpose of the corporate brand to which they belong.

   a. Channel conflict
   b. Corporate colours
   c. Status brand
   d. Brand architecture

10. _____ is an advertisement in which a particular product specifically mentions a competitor by name for the express purpose of showing why the competitor is inferior to the product naming it.

This should not be confused with parody advertisements, where a fictional product is being advertised for the purpose of poking fun at the particular advertisement, nor should it be confused with the use of a coined brand name for the purpose of comparing the product without actually naming an actual competitor. ('Wikipedia tastes better and is less filling than the Encyclopedia Galactica.')

In the 1980s, during what has been referred to as the cola wars, soft-drink manufacturer Pepsi ran a series of advertisements where people, caught on hidden camera, in a blind taste test, chose Pepsi over rival Coca-Cola.

   a. GL-70
   b. Heavy-up
   c. Cost per conversion
   d. Comparative advertising

11. _____ is an Internet-based marketing practice in which a business rewards one or more affiliates for each visitor or customer brought about by the affiliate's marketing efforts.

_____ is also the name of the industry where a number of different types of companies and individuals are performing this form of Internet marketing, including affiliate networks, affiliate management companies, and in-house affiliate managers, specialized third party vendors, and various types of affiliates/publishers who promote the products and services of their partners.

_____ overlaps with other Internet marketing methods to some degree, because affiliates often use regular advertising methods.

Chapter 8. Traffic Building

a. ADTECH
b. AMAX
c. ACNielsen
d. Affiliate marketing

12. _____ is a market coverage strategy in which a firm decides to ignore market segment differences and go after the whole market with one offer.it is type of marketing (or attempting to sell through persuasion) of a product to a wide audience. The idea is to broadcast a message that will reach the largest number of people possible. Traditionally _____ has focused on radio, television and newspapers as the medium used to reach this broad audience.

a. Mass marketing
b. Cyberdoc
c. Business-to-consumer
d. Marketspace

13. _____ is a term used to denote a section of the media specifically designed to reach a very large audience such as the population of a nation state. It was coined in the 1920s with the advent of nationwide radio networks, mass-circulation newspapers and magazines, although _____ were present centuries before the term became common. The term public media has a similar meaning: it is the sum of the public mass distributors of news and entertainment across media such as newspapers, television, radio, broadcasting, which may require union membership in some large markets such as Newspaper Guild, AFTRA, ' text publishers.

a. 180SearchAssistant
b. Mass media
c. Power III
d. 6-3-5 Brainwriting

14. _____ is the deliberate attempt to manage the public's perception of a subject. The subjects of _____ include people (for example, politicians and performing artists), goods and services, organizations of all kinds, and works of art or entertainment.

From a marketing perspective, _____ is one component of promotion.

a. Little value placed on potential benefits
b. Brando
c. Pearson's chi-square
d. Publicity

Chapter 8. Traffic Building

15. _____ refer to a collection of facts usually collected as the result of experience, observation or experiment or a set of premises. This may consist of numbers, words particularly as measurements or observations of a set of variables. _____ are often viewed as a lowest level of abstraction from which information and knowledge are derived.
    a. Pearson product-moment correlation coefficient
    b. Sample size
    c. Data
    d. Mean

16. In economics, business, retail, and accounting, a _____ is the value of money that has been used up to produce something, and hence is not available for use anymore. In economics, a _____ is an alternative that is given up as a result of a decision. In business, the _____ may be one of acquisition, in which case the amount of money expended to acquire it is counted as _____.
    a. Variable cost
    b. Transaction cost
    c. Fixed costs
    d. Cost

17. _____, often abbreviated to _____, is a phrase often used in online advertising and marketing related to web traffic. It is used for measuring the worth and cost of a specific e-marketing campaign. This technique is applied with web banners, text links, e-mail spam, and opt-in e-mail advertising, although opt-in e-mail advertising is more commonly charged on a cost per action (CPA) basis.
    a. Cost per time
    b. Cost per mille
    c. Frequency capping
    d. Cost per impression

18. In marketing, customer _____, lifetime customer value (LCV), or _____ (LTV) and a new concept of 'customer life cycle management' is the present value of the future cash flows attributed to the customer relationship. Use of customer _____ as a marketing metric tends to place greater emphasis on customer service and long-term customer satisfaction, rather than on maximizing short-term sales.

Customer _____ has intuitive appeal as a marketing concept, because in theory it represents exactly how much each customer is worth in monetary terms, and therefore exactly how much a marketing department should be willing to spend to acquire each customer.

a. Sweepstakes
b. Brand infiltration
c. Lifetime value
d. Value chain

19. In economics, _____ is the process by which a firm determines the price and output level that returns the greatest profit. There are several approaches to this problem. The total revenue--total cost method relies on the fact that profit equals revenue minus cost, and the marginal revenue--marginal cost method is based on the fact that total profit in a perfectly competitive market reaches its maximum point where marginal revenue equals marginal cost.
   a. 180SearchAssistant
   b. Profit maximization
   c. Power III
   d. Profit margin

20. In economics, _____ is the ratio of the percent change in one variable to the percent change in another variable. It is a tool for measuring the responsiveness of a function to changes in parameters in a relative way. Commonly analyzed are _____ of substitution, price and wealth.
   a. Opinion leadership
   b. Intellectual property
   c. ACNielsen
   d. Elasticity

21. _____ in economics and business is the result of an exchange and from that trade we assign a numerical monetary value to a good, service or asset. If I trade 4 apples for an orange, the _____ of an orange is 4 - apples. Inversely, the _____ of an apple is 1/4 oranges.
   a. Contribution margin-based pricing
   b. Price
   c. Discounts and allowances
   d. Pricing

22. _____ is a term used to describe a process of preparing and collecting data - for example as part of a process improvement or similar project.

_____ usually takes place early on in an improvement project, and is often formalised through a _____ Plan which often contains the following activity.

1. Pre collection activity - Agree goals, target data, definitions, methods
2. Collection - _____
3. Present Findings - usually involves some form of sorting analysis and/or presentation.

A formal _____ process is necessary as it ensures that data gathered is both defined and accurate and that subsequent decisions based on arguments embodied in the findings are valid . The process provides both a baseline from which to measure from and in certain cases a target on what to improve. Types of _____ 1-By mail questionnaires 2-By personal interview

- Six sigma
- Sampling (statistics)

a. Data collection
b. 180SearchAssistant
c. Power III
d. 6-3-5 Brainwriting

23. _____ is systematic determination of merit, worth, and significance of something or someone using criteria against a set of standards. _____ often is used to characterize and appraise subjects of interest in a wide range of human enterprises, including the arts, criminal justice, foundations and non-profit organizations, government, health care, and other human services.

Depending on the topic of interest, there are professional groups which look to the quality and rigor of the _____ process.

a. ACNielsen
b. Evaluation
c. AMAX
d. ADTECH

24. _____ is a way of measuring the success of an online advertising campaign. A CTR is obtained by dividing the number of users who clicked on an ad on a web page by the number of times the ad was delivered (impressions.) For example, if a banner ad was delivered 100 times (impressions delivered) and one person clicked on it (clicks recorded), then the resulting CTR would be 1 percent.

Chapter 8. Traffic Building

a. JICIMS
b. Web analytics
c. Display advertising
d. Click-through rate

25. A _____ or banner ad is a form of advertising on the World Wide Web. This form of online advertising entails embedding an advertisement into a web page. It is intended to attract traffic to a website by linking to the website of the advertiser.
   a. Disintermediation
   b. Spamvertising
   c. Consumer privacy
   d. Web banner

26. Competitiveness is a comparative concept of the ability and performance of a firm, sub-sector or country to sell and supply goods and/or services in a given market. Although widely used in economics and business management, the usefulness of the concept, particularly in the context of national competitiveness, is vigorously disputed by economists, such as Paul Krugman .

The term may also be applied to markets, where it is used to refer to the extent to which the market structure may be regarded as perfectly _____.

   a. Free trade zone
   b. Customs union
   c. Geographical pricing
   d. Competitive

27. _____ is a broad label that refers to any individuals or households that use goods and services generated within the economy. The concept of a _____ is used in different contexts, so that the usage and significance of the term may vary.

A _____ is a person who uses any product or service.

   a. 6-3-5 Brainwriting
   b. Power III
   c. 180SearchAssistant
   d. Consumer

28. _____ is a magazine, delivering news, analysis and data on marketing and media. The magazine was started as a broadsheet newspaper in Chicago in 1930. Today, its content appears in a print weekly distributed around the world and on many electronic platforms, including: AdAge.com, daily e-mail newsletters called Ad Age Daily, Ad Age's Mediaworks and Ad Age Digital; weekly newsletters such as Madison ' Vine (about branded entertainment) and Ad Age China; podcasts called Why It Matters and various videos.

   a. Ethical Consumer
   b. Outsert
   c. Advertising Age
   d. Adweek

29. _____ refers to several different marketing arrangements:

_____ is when two companies form an alliance to work together, creating marketing synergy. As described in _____: The Science of Alliance:

_____ is an arrangement that associates a single product or service with more than one brand name, or otherwise associates a product with someone other than the principal producer. The typical _____ agreement involves two or more companies acting in cooperation to associate any of various logos, color schemes, or brand identifiers to a specific product that is contractually designated for this purpose.

   a. Target audience
   b. Co-branding
   c. Line extension
   d. Brand Development Index

Chapter 9. Personalization

1. _____ is a list for goods and materials held available in stock by a business. It is also used for a list of the contents of a household and for a list for testamentary purposes of the possessions of someone who has died. In accounting _____ is considered an asset.

   a. Ending Inventory
   b. ADTECH
   c. ACNielsen
   d. Inventory

2. The _____ is an equation that equals the cost of goods sold divided by the average inventory. Average inventory equals beginning inventory plus ending inventory divided by 2.

   The formula for _____:

   $$\text{Inventory Turnover} = \frac{\text{Cost of Goods Sold}}{\text{Average Inventory}}$$

   The formula for average inventory:

   $$\text{Average Inventory} = \frac{\text{Beginning inventory} + \text{Ending inventory}}{2}$$

   A low turnover rate may point to overstocking, obsolescence, or deficiencies in the product line or marketing effort.

   a. ADTECH
   b. AMAX
   c. ACNielsen
   d. Inventory turnover

3. _____ or personalisation is tailoring a consumer product, electronic or written medium to a user based on personal details or characteristics they provide. More recently, it has especially been applied in the context of the World Wide Web.

   Web pages are personalized based on the interests of an individual.

   a. Complex sale
   b. Sexism,
   c. Flighting
   d. Personalization

Chapter 9. Personalization

4. _____ in organizations and public policy is both the organizational process of creating and maintaining a plan; and the psychological process of thinking about the activities required to create a desired goal on some scale. As such, it is a fundamental property of intelligent behavior. This thought process is essential to the creation and refinement of a plan, or integration of it with other plans, that is, it combines forecasting of developments with the preparation of scenarios of how to react to them.
   a. Planning
   b. Power III
   c. 6-3-5 Brainwriting
   d. 180SearchAssistant

5. On an intranet or B2E Enterprise Web portals, personalization is often based on user attributes such as department, functional area, or role. The term _____ in this context refers to the ability of users to modify the page layout or specify what content should be displayed.

There are two categories of personalizations:

   1. Rule-based
   2. Content-based

Web personalization models include rules-based filtering, based on 'if this, then that' rules processing, and collaborative filtering, which serves relevant material to customers by combining their own personal preferences with the preferences of like-minded others. Collaborative filtering works well for books, music, video, etc.

   a. Movin'
   b. Self branding
   c. Cashmere Agency
   d. Customization

6. _____. People may not recognize the value in offered personalization, such as when firms offer to customize product offers. Many people don't want to receive any such offers, period.
   a. Push
   b. Bottling lines
   c. Category Development Index
   d. Little value placed on potential benefits

7. _____ is an advertisement in which a particular product specifically mentions a competitor by name for the express purpose of showing why the competitor is inferior to the product naming it.

This should not be confused with parody advertisements, where a fictional product is being advertised for the purpose of poking fun at the particular advertisement, nor should it be confused with the use of a coined brand name for the purpose of comparing the product without actually naming an actual competitor. ('Wikipedia tastes better and is less filling than the Encyclopedia Galactica.')

In the 1980s, during what has been referred to as the cola wars, soft-drink manufacturer Pepsi ran a series of advertisements where people, caught on hidden camera, in a blind taste test, chose Pepsi over rival Coca-Cola.

  a. Heavy-up
  b. Cost per conversion
  c. Comparative advertising
  d. GL-70

8. In marketing, _____ is the process of distinguishing the differences of a product or offering from others, to make it more attractive to a particular target market. This involves differentiating it from competitors' products as well as one's own product offerings.

Differentiation is a source of competitive advantage.

  a. Product differentiation
  b. Corporate image
  c. Marketing myopia
  d. Packshot

9. Diminishing returns can be divided into three categories: 1. Diminishing Total returns, which implies reduction in _____ with every additional unit of input. This occurs after point A in the graph. 2. Diminishing Average returns, which refers to the portion of the APP curve after its intersection with MPP curve. 3. Diminishing Marginal returns, refers to the point where the MPP curve starts to slope down and travels all the way down to the x-axis and beyond. Putting it in a chronological order, at first the marginal returns start to diminish, then the average returns, followed finally by the total returns.
  a. 180SearchAssistant
  b. Power III
  c. 6-3-5 Brainwriting
  d. Total product

Chapter 9. Personalization

10. _____ is a form of communication that typically attempts to persuade potential customers to purchase or to consume more of a particular brand of product or service. 'While now central to the contemporary global economy and the reproduction of global production networks, it is only quite recently that _____ has been more than a marginal influence on patterns of sales and production. The formation of modern _____ was intimately bound up with the emergence of new forms of monopoly capitalism around the end of the 19th and beginning of the 20th century as one element in corporate strategies to create, organize and where possible control markets, especially for mass produced consumer goods.

   a. AMAX
   b. ACNielsen
   c. ADTECH
   d. Advertising

11. _____ is a form of promotion that uses the Internet and World Wide Web for the expressed purpose of delivering marketing messages to attract customers. Examples of _____ include contextual ads on search engine results pages, banner ads, Rich Media Ads, Social network advertising, online classified advertising, advertising networks and e-mail marketing, including e-mail spam.

   Online video directories for brands are a good example of interactive advertising.

   a. ACNielsen
   b. ADTECH
   c. AMAX
   d. Online advertising

12. An _____ is the manufacturing of a good or service within a category. Although _____ is a broad term for any kind of economic production, in economics and urban planning _____ is a synonym for the secondary sector, which is a type of economic activity involved in the manufacturing of raw materials into goods and products.

   There are four key industrial economic sectors: the primary sector, largely raw material extraction industries such as mining and farming; the secondary sector, involving refining, construction, and manufacturing; the tertiary sector, which deals with services (such as law and medicine) and distribution of manufactured goods; and the quaternary sector, a relatively new type of knowledge _____ focusing on technological research, design and development such as computer programming, and biochemistry.

   a. Industry
   b. AMAX
   c. ACNielsen
   d. ADTECH

Chapter 9. Personalization

13. In economics, business, retail, and accounting, a _____ is the value of money that has been used up to produce something, and hence is not available for use anymore. In economics, a _____ is an alternative that is given up as a result of a decision. In business, the _____ may be one of acquisition, in which case the amount of money expended to acquire it is counted as _____.
    a. Cost
    b. Fixed costs
    c. Transaction cost
    d. Variable cost

14. Switching barriers or _____s are terms used in microeconomics, strategic management, and marketing to describe any impediment to a customer's changing of suppliers.

    In many markets, consumers are forced to incur costs when switching from one supplier to another. These costs are called _____s and can come in many different shapes.

    a. Strategic business unit
    b. Strategic group
    c. Chaotics
    d. Switching cost

15. _____, also referred to as i-marketing, web marketing, online marketing is the marketing of products or services over the Internet.

    The Internet has brought many unique benefits to marketing, one of which being lower costs for the distribution of information and media to a global audience. The interactive nature of _____, both in terms of providing instant response and eliciting responses, is a unique quality of the medium.

    a. ADTECH
    b. Internet marketing
    c. ACNielsen
    d. AMAX

16. _____ is a form of Internet marketing that seeks to promote websites by increasing their visibility in search engine result pages (SERPs.) According to the _____ Professional Organization, _____ methods include: search engine optimization (or SEO), paid placement, contextual advertising, and paid inclusion. Other sources, including the New York Times, define _____ as the practice of buying paid search listings.

a. Display advertising
b. Blog marketing
c. Pay for placement
d. Search engine marketing

17. _____ is defined by the American _____ Association as the activity, set of institutions, and processes for creating, communicating, delivering, and exchanging offerings that have value for customers, clients, partners, and society at large. The term developed from the original meaning which referred literally to going to market, as in shopping, or going to a market to sell goods or services.

_____ practice tends to be seen as a creative industry, which includes advertising, distribution and selling.

a. Marketing myopia
b. Product naming
c. Customer acquisition management
d. Marketing

18. _____ is a market coverage strategy in which a firm decides to ignore market segment differences and go after the whole market with one offer.it is type of marketing (or attempting to sell through persuasion) of a product to a wide audience. The idea is to broadcast a message that will reach the largest number of people possible. Traditionally _____ has focused on radio, television and newspapers as the medium used to reach this broad audience.

a. Business-to-consumer
b. Cyberdoc
c. Mass marketing
d. Marketspace

19. _____, in marketing, manufacturing, and management, is the use of flexible computer-aided manufacturing systems to produce custom output. Those systems combine the low unit costs of mass production processes with the flexibility of individual customization.

'_____' is the new frontier in business competition for both manufacturing and service industries.

a. Flanking marketing warfare strategies
b. Vertical integration
c. Power III
d. Mass customization

Chapter 9. Personalization

20. _____s form a specific type of information filtering (IF) technique that attempts to present information items (movies, music, books, news, images, web pages, etc.) that are likely of interest to the user. Typically, a _____ compares the user's profile to some reference characteristics, and seeks to predict the 'rating' that a user would give to an item they had not yet considered.
   a. Locator software
   b. Recommender system
   c. Permission marketing
   d. Spamvertising

21. A personal and cultural _____ is a relative ethic _____, an assumption upon which implementation can be extrapolated. A _____ system is a set of consistent _____s and measures that is soo not true. A principle _____ is a foundation upon which other _____s and measures of integrity are based.
   a. Value
   b. Package-on-Package
   c. Supreme Court of the United States
   d. Perceptual maps

22. _____ is a form of marketing developed from direct response marketing campaigns conducted in the 1970's and 1980's which emphasizes customer retention and satisfaction, rather than a dominant focus on 'point of sale' transactions.

   _____ differs from other forms of marketing in that it recognizes the long term value to the firm of keeping customers, as opposed to direct or 'Intrusion' marketing, which focuses upon acquisition of new clients by targeting majority demographics based upon prospective client lists.

   _____ refers to long-term and mutually beneficial arrangement wherein both buyer and seller focus on value enhancement through the certain of more satisfying exchange.This approach attempts to transcend the simple purchase exchange process with customer to make more meaningful and richer contact by providing a more holistic, personalized purchase, and use orn consumption experience to create stronger ties.

   a. Global marketing
   b. Guerrilla Marketing
   c. Diversity marketing
   d. Relationship marketing

23. In statistics, an _____ is a term in a statistical model added when the effect of two or more variables is not simply additive. Such a term reflects that the effect of one variable depends on the values of one or more other variables.

Thus, for a response Y and two variables x_1 and x_2 an additive model would be:

$$Y = ax_1 + bx_2 + \text{error}$$

In contrast to this,

$$Y = ax_1 + bx_2 + c(x_1 \times x_2) + \text{error},$$

is an example of a model with an _____ between variables x_1 and x_2 ('error' refers to the random variable whose value by which y differs from the expected value of y.)

   a. ACNielsen
   b. ADTECH
   c. AMAX
   d. Interaction

24. _____ is a recursive process where two or more people or organizations work together toward an intersection of common goals -- for example, an intellectual endeavor that is creative in nature--by sharing knowledge, learning and building consensus. _____ does not require leadership and can sometimes bring better results through decentralization and egalitarianism. In particular, teams that work collaboratively can obtain greater resources, recognition and reward when facing competition for finite resources._____ is also present in opposing goals exhibiting the notion of adversarial _____, though this notion is atypical of the annotation that people have given towards their understanding of _____.
   a. Power III
   b. 180SearchAssistant
   c. 6-3-5 Brainwriting
   d. Collaboration

25. _____ is the process of filtering for information or patterns using techniques involving collaboration among multiple agents, viewpoints, data sources, etc. Applications of _____ typically involve very large data sets. _____ methods have been applied to many different kinds of data including sensing and monitoring data - such as in mineral exploration, environmental sensing over large areas or multiple sensors; financial data - such as financial service institutions that integrate many financial sources; or in electronic commerce and web 2.0 applications where the focus is on user data, etc.
   a. 6-3-5 Brainwriting
   b. Power III
   c. 180SearchAssistant
   d. Collaborative filtering

26. _____ refer to a collection of facts usually collected as the result of experience, observation or experiment or a set of premises. This may consist of numbers, words particularly as measurements or observations of a set of variables. _____ are often viewed as a lowest level of abstraction from which information and knowledge are derived.
   a. Pearson product-moment correlation coefficient
   b. Mean
   c. Sample size
   d. Data

27. In the mathematical discipline of graph theory a _____ or edge-independent set in a graph is a set of edges without common vertices. It may also be an entire graph consisting of edges without common vertices.

Given a graph G = (V,E), a _____ M in G is a set of pairwise non-adjacent edges; that is, no two edges share a common vertex.

   a. 180SearchAssistant
   b. Power III
   c. 6-3-5 Brainwriting
   d. Matching

28. _____ is a form of social influence. It is the process of guiding people toward the adoption of an idea, attitude, or action by rational and symbolic (though not always logical) means. It is strategy of problem-solving relying on 'appeals' rather than coercion.
   a. 180SearchAssistant
   b. Power III
   c. 6-3-5 Brainwriting
   d. Persuasion

29. _____ was a writer, management consultant, and self-described 'social ecologist.' Widely considered to be the father of 'modern management,' his 39 books and countless scholarly and popular articles explored how humans are organized across all sectors of society--in business, government and the nonprofit world. His writings have predicted many of the major developments of the late twentieth century, including privatization and decentralization; the rise of Japan to economic world power; the decisive importance of marketing; and the emergence of the information society with its necessity of lifelong learning. In 1959, Drucker coined the term 'knowledge worker' and later in his life considered knowledge work productivity to be the next frontier of management.
   a. Nouveau riche
   b. Peter Ferdinand Drucker
   c. Rick Boyce
   d. Paschal Eze

Chapter 10. Creating Commitment

1. _____ are used for a variety of social and professional groups interacting via the Internet. It does not necessarily mean that there is a strong bond among the members, although Howard Rheingold, author of the book of the same name, mentions that _____ form 'when people carry on public discussions long enough, with sufficient human feeling, to form webs of personal relationships'. An email distribution list may have hundreds of members and the communication which takes place may be merely informational (questions and answers are posted), but members may remain relative strangers and the membership turnover rate could be high.

    a. Power III
    b. Virtual communities
    c. 6-3-5 Brainwriting
    d. 180SearchAssistant

2. _____ is a social networking website with an interactive, user-submitted network of friends, personal profiles, blogs, groups, photos, music, and videos for teenagers and adults internationally. Its headquarters are in Beverly Hills, California, USA, where it shares an office building with its immediate owner, Fox Interactive Media; which is owned by News Corporation, which has its headquarters in New York City. In June 2006, _____ was the most popular social networking site in the United States.

    a. Fountain Fresh International
    b. Chief marketing officer
    c. National Asset Recovery Services
    d. MySpace

3. _____ describes the situation when output from (or information about the result of) an event or phenomenon in the past will influence the same event/phenomenon in the present or future. When an event is part of a chain of cause-and-effect that forms a circuit or loop, then the event is said to 'feed back' into itself.

    _____ is also a synonym for:

    - _____ Signal; the information about the initial event that is the basis for subsequent modification of the event.
    - _____ Loop; the causal path that leads from the initial generation of the _____ signal to the subsequent modification of the event.

    _____ is a mechanism, process or signal that is looped back to control a system within itself. Such a loop is called a _____ loop.

    a. 6-3-5 Brainwriting
    b. Feedback
    c. Power III
    d. 180SearchAssistant

Chapter 10. Creating Commitment

4. _____ is an advertisement in which a particular product specifically mentions a competitor by name for the express purpose of showing why the competitor is inferior to the product naming it.

This should not be confused with parody advertisements, where a fictional product is being advertised for the purpose of poking fun at the particular advertisement, nor should it be confused with the use of a coined brand name for the purpose of comparing the product without actually naming an actual competitor. ('Wikipedia tastes better and is less filling than the Encyclopedia Galactica.')

In the 1980s, during what has been referred to as the cola wars, soft-drink manufacturer Pepsi ran a series of advertisements where people, caught on hidden camera, in a blind taste test, chose Pepsi over rival Coca-Cola.

a. GL-70
b. Heavy-up
c. Cost per conversion
d. Comparative advertising

5. _____ is a form of communication that typically attempts to persuade potential customers to purchase or to consume more of a particular brand of product or service. 'While now central to the contemporary global economy and the reproduction of global production networks, it is only quite recently that _____ has been more than a marginal influence on patterns of sales and production. The formation of modern _____ was intimately bound up with the emergence of new forms of monopoly capitalism around the end of the 19th and beginning of the 20th century as one element in corporate strategies to create, organize and where possible control markets, especially for mass produced consumer goods.

a. ADTECH
b. AMAX
c. ACNielsen
d. Advertising

6. In statistics, an _____ is a term in a statistical model added when the effect of two or more variables is not simply additive. Such a term reflects that the effect of one variable depends on the values of one or more other variables.

Thus, for a response Y and two variables x_1 and x_2 an additive model would be:

$$Y = ax_1 + bx_2 + \text{error}$$

In contrast to this,

$$Y = ax_1 + bx_2 + c(x_1 \times x_2) + \text{error},$$

is an example of a model with an _____ between variables x_1 and x_2 ('error' refers to the random variable whose value by which y differs from the expected value of y.)

a. AMAX
b. ACNielsen
c. ADTECH
d. Interaction

7. The _____ is the group of customers and/or consumers that a business serves. In the most situations, a large part of this group is made up of repeat customers with a high ratio of purchase over time. These customers are the main source of consumer spending.
   a. First-mover advantage
   b. Customer base
   c. Psychological pricing
   d. Supplier diversity

8. _____, also referred to as i-marketing, web marketing, online marketing is the marketing of products or services over the Internet.

The Internet has brought many unique benefits to marketing, one of which being lower costs for the distribution of information and media to a global audience. The interactive nature of _____, both in terms of providing instant response and eliciting responses, is a unique quality of the medium.

   a. ACNielsen
   b. AMAX
   c. Internet marketing
   d. ADTECH

9. _____ is a form of Internet marketing that seeks to promote websites by increasing their visibility in search engine result pages (SERPs.) According to the _____ Professional Organization, _____ methods include: search engine optimization (or SEO), paid placement, contextual advertising, and paid inclusion. Other sources, including the New York Times, define _____ as the practice of buying paid search listings.
   a. Display advertising
   b. Pay for placement
   c. Blog marketing
   d. Search engine marketing

10. _____ is defined by the American _____ Association as the activity, set of institutions, and processes for creating, communicating, delivering, and exchanging offerings that have value for customers, clients, partners, and society at large. The term developed from the original meaning which referred literally to going to market, as in shopping, or going to a market to sell goods or services.

Chapter 10. Creating Commitment

_____ practice tends to be seen as a creative industry, which includes advertising, distribution and selling.

a. Marketing myopia
b. Customer acquisition management
c. Product naming
d. Marketing

11. The loyalty business model is a business model used in strategic management in which company resources are employed so as to increase the loyalty of customers and other stakeholders in the expectation that corporate objectives will be met or surpassed. A typical example of this type of model is: quality of product or service leads to customer satisfaction, which leads to _____, which leads to profitability.

Fredrick Reichheld (1996) expanded the loyalty business model beyond customers and employees.

a. 180SearchAssistant
b. Power III
c. 6-3-5 Brainwriting
d. Customer loyalty

12. _____s are structured marketing efforts that reward, and therefore encourage, loyal buying behaviour -- behaviour which is potentially of benefit to the firm.

In marketing generally and in retailing more specifically, a loyalty card, rewards card, points card, advantage card, or club card is a plastic or paper card, visually similar to a credit card or debit card, that identifies the card holder as a member in a _____. Loyalty cards are a system of the loyalty business model.

a. Power III
b. 6-3-5 Brainwriting
c. Loyalty program
d. 180SearchAssistant

13. A _____ is a single page leaflet advertising a nightclub, event, service, or other activity. _____s are typically used by individuals or businesses to promote their products or services. They are a form of mass marketing or small scale, community communication.

a. Consumption Map
b. Just-In-Case
c. Quantitative
d. Flyer

14. In economics, business, retail, and accounting, a _____ is the value of money that has been used up to produce something, and hence is not available for use anymore. In economics, a _____ is an alternative that is given up as a result of a decision. In business, the _____ may be one of acquisition, in which case the amount of money expended to acquire it is counted as _____.

a. Transaction cost
b. Variable cost
c. Fixed costs
d. Cost

15. Switching barriers or _____s are terms used in microeconomics, strategic management, and marketing to describe any impediment to a customer's changing of suppliers.

In many markets, consumers are forced to incur costs when switching from one supplier to another. These costs are called _____s and can come in many different shapes.

a. Chaotics
b. Strategic group
c. Switching cost
d. Strategic business unit

Chapter 11. Innovation and the Net

1. _____ refer to a collection of facts usually collected as the result of experience, observation or experiment or a set of premises. This may consist of numbers, words particularly as measurements or observations of a set of variables. _____ are often viewed as a lowest level of abstraction from which information and knowledge are derived.
   a. Pearson product-moment correlation coefficient
   b. Data
   c. Sample size
   d. Mean

2. In business and engineering, new _____ is the term used to describe the complete process of bringing a new product or service to market. There are two parallel paths involved in the Nproduct development process: one involves the idea generation, product design, and detail engineering; the other involves market research and marketing analysis. Companies typically see new _____ as the first stage in generating and commercializing new products within the overall strategic process of product life cycle management used to maintain or grow their market share.
   a. New product screening
   b. New product development
   c. Specification tree
   d. Product development

3. _____ is one of the four elements of marketing mix. An organization or set of organizations (go-betweens) involved in the process of making a product or service available for use or consumption by a consumer or business user.

   The other three parts of the marketing mix are product, pricing, and promotion.

   a. Japan Advertising Photographers' Association
   b. Distribution
   c. Better Living Through Chemistry
   d. Comparison-Shopping agent

4. _____, also referred to as i-marketing, web marketing, online marketing is the marketing of products or services over the Internet.

   The Internet has brought many unique benefits to marketing, one of which being lower costs for the distribution of information and media to a global audience. The interactive nature of _____, both in terms of providing instant response and eliciting responses, is a unique quality of the medium.

   a. ADTECH
   b. AMAX
   c. ACNielsen
   d. Internet marketing

5. _____ is a form of Internet marketing that seeks to promote websites by increasing their visibility in search engine result pages (SERPs.) According to the _____ Professional Organization, _____ methods include: search engine optimization (or SEO), paid placement, contextual advertising, and paid inclusion. Other sources, including the New York Times, define _____ as the practice of buying paid search listings.
   a. Display advertising
   b. Blog marketing
   c. Pay for placement
   d. Search engine marketing

6. _____ is defined by the American _____ Association as the activity, set of institutions, and processes for creating, communicating, delivering, and exchanging offerings that have value for customers, clients, partners, and society at large. The term developed from the original meaning which referred literally to going to market, as in shopping, or going to a market to sell goods or services.

   _____ practice tends to be seen as a creative industry, which includes advertising, distribution and selling.

   a. Product naming
   b. Marketing myopia
   c. Customer acquisition management
   d. Marketing

7. A _____ is a process that can allow an organization to concentrate its limited resources on the greatest opportunities to increase sales and achieve a sustainable competitive advantage. A _____ should be centered around the key concept that customer satisfaction is the main goal.

   A _____ is most effective when it is an integral component of corporate strategy, defining how the organization will successfully engage customers, prospects, and competitors in the market arena.

   a. Cyberdoc
   b. Marketing strategy
   c. Psychographic
   d. Societal marketing

8. A _____ is a plan of action designed to achieve a particular goal.

   _____ is different from tactics. In military terms, tactics is concerned with the conduct of an engagement while _____ is concerned with how different engagements are linked.

a. 180SearchAssistant
b. 6-3-5 Brainwriting
c. Power III
d. Strategy

9. _____ is a rivalry between individuals, groups, nations for territory, a niche, or allocation of resources. It arises whenever two or more parties strive for a goal which cannot be shared. _____ occurs naturally between living organisms which co-exist in the same environment.

a. Non-price competition
b. Price competition
c. Price fixing
d. Competition

10. _____ is a statistical technique used in market research to determine how people value different features that make up an individual product or service.

The objective of _____ is to determine what combination of a limited number of attributes is most influential on respondent choice or decision making. A controlled set of potential products or services is shown to respondents and by analyzing how they make preferences between these products, the implicit valuation of the individual elements making up the product or service can be determined.

a. Power III
b. Likert scale
c. Semantic differential
d. Conjoint analysis

11. _____ is a broad label that refers to any individuals or households that use goods and services generated within the economy. The concept of a _____ is used in different contexts, so that the usage and significance of the term may vary.

A _____ is a person who uses any product or service.

a. Consumer
b. Power III
c. 6-3-5 Brainwriting
d. 180SearchAssistant

12. A _____ is a form of qualitative research in which a group of people are asked about their attitude towards a product, service, concept, advertisement, idea, or packaging. Questions are asked in an interactive group setting where participants are free to talk with other group members.

Ernest Dichter originated the idea of having a 'group therapy' for products and this process is what became known as a _____.

  a. Focus group
  b. Marketing research process
  c. Logit analysis
  d. Cross tabulation

13. _____ is the examining of goods or services from retailers with the intent to purchase at that time. _____ is an activity of selection and/or purchase. In some contexts it is considered a leisure activity as well as an economic one.
  a. Discount store
  b. Hawkers
  c. Khodebshchik
  d. Shopping

14. _____ often refers to either primary or secondary research. Secondary research involves a company using information compiled from various sources, which is about a new or existing product. The advantages of secondary research are that it is relatively cheap and easily accessible.
  a. Mystery shoppers
  b. Mystery shopping
  c. Questionnaire
  d. Market research

15. In economics, _____ is the desire to own something and the ability to pay for it. The term _____ signifies the ability or the willingness to buy a particular commodity at a given point of time.

  a. Market system
  b. Market dominance
  c. Discretionary spending
  d. Demand

16. 'Speaking generally, properties are those physical quantities which directly describe the physical attributes of the system; _____s are those combinations of the properties which suffice to determine the response of the system. Properties can have all sorts of dimensions, depending upon the system being considered; _____s are dimensionless, or have the dimension of time or its reciprocal.'

The term can also be used in engineering contexts, however, as it is typically used in the physical sciences.

When the terms formal _____ and actual _____ are used, they generally correspond with the definitions used in computer science.

   a. 6-3-5 Brainwriting
   b. 180SearchAssistant
   c. Parameter
   d. Power III

17. _____ describes the situation when output from (or information about the result of) an event or phenomenon in the past will influence the same event/phenomenon in the present or future. When an event is part of a chain of cause-and-effect that forms a circuit or loop, then the event is said to 'feed back' into itself.

_____ is also a synonym for:

- _____ Signal; the information about the initial event that is the basis for subsequent modification of the event.
- _____ Loop; the causal path that leads from the initial generation of the _____ signal to the subsequent modification of the event.

_____ is a mechanism, process or signal that is looped back to control a system within itself. Such a loop is called a _____ loop.

   a. Power III
   b. 180SearchAssistant
   c. 6-3-5 Brainwriting
   d. Feedback

18. A _____ is a collection of symbols, experiences and associations connected with a product, a service, a person or any other artifact or entity.

_____s have become increasingly important components of culture and the economy, now being described as 'cultural accessories and personal philosophies'.

Some people distinguish the psychological aspect of a _____ from the experiential aspect.

a. Brandable software
b. Brand equity
c. Store brand
d. Brand

19. _____ refers to the marketing effects or outcomes that accrue to a product with its brand name compared with those that would accrue if the same product did not have the brand name . And, at the root of these marketing effects is consumers' knowledge. In other words, consumers' knowledge about a brand makes manufacturers/advertisers respond differently or adopt appropriately adapt measures for the marketing of the brand .

a. Brand aversion
b. Product extension
c. Brand equity
d. Brand image

Chapter 12. Pricing in an Online World

1. _____ in economics and business is the result of an exchange and from that trade we assign a numerical monetary value to a good, service or asset. If I trade 4 apples for an orange, the _____ of an orange is 4 - apples. Inversely, the _____ of an apple is 1/4 oranges.
   a. Contribution margin-based pricing
   b. Pricing
   c. Discounts and allowances
   d. Price

2. _____ is one of the four Ps of the marketing mix. The other three aspects are product, promotion, and place. It is also a key variable in microeconomic price allocation theory.
   a. Competitor indexing
   b. Relationship based pricing
   c. Price
   d. Pricing

3. In economics, _____ is the ratio of the percent change in one variable to the percent change in another variable. It is a tool for measuring the responsiveness of a function to changes in parameters in a relative way. Commonly analyzed are _____ of substitution, price and wealth.
   a. ACNielsen
   b. Intellectual property
   c. Opinion leadership
   d. Elasticity

4. _____ is a marketing strategy that involves offering several products for sale as one combined product. This strategy is very common in the software business (for example: bundle a word processor, a spreadsheet, and a database into a single office suite), in the cable television industry (for example, basic cable in the United States generally offers many channels at one price), and in the fast food industry in which multiple items are combined into a complete meal. A bundle of products is sometimes referred to as a package deal or a compilation or an anthology.
   a. Primary research
   b. Product bundling
   c. Psychographic
   d. Technology acceptance model

5. In economics and finance, _____ is the change in total cost that arises when the quantity produced changes by one unit. It is the cost of producing one more unit of a good. Mathematically, the _____ function is expressed as the first derivative of the total cost (TC) function with respect to quantity (Q.)

a. Transaction cost
b. Fixed costs
c. Variable cost
d. Marginal cost

6. In microeconomics, _____ is the extra revenue that an additional unit of product will bring. It is the additional income from selling one more unit of a good; sometimes equal to price. It can also be described as the change in total revenue/change in number of units sold.
   a. Hoarding
   b. Product proliferation
   c. Marginal revenue
   d. Total cost

7. In economics, _____ is the process by which a firm determines the price and output level that returns the greatest profit. There are several approaches to this problem. The total revenue--total cost method relies on the fact that profit equals revenue minus cost, and the marginal revenue--marginal cost method is based on the fact that total profit in a perfectly competitive market reaches its maximum point where marginal revenue equals marginal cost.
   a. 180SearchAssistant
   b. Power III
   c. Profit margin
   d. Profit maximization

8. In economics, business, retail, and accounting, a _____ is the value of money that has been used up to produce something, and hence is not available for use anymore. In economics, a _____ is an alternative that is given up as a result of a decision. In business, the _____ may be one of acquisition, in which case the amount of money expended to acquire it is counted as _____.
   a. Variable cost
   b. Cost
   c. Transaction cost
   d. Fixed costs

9. _____ is a form of communication that typically attempts to persuade potential customers to purchase or to consume more of a particular brand of product or service. 'While now central to the contemporary global economy and the reproduction of global production networks, it is only quite recently that _____ has been more than a marginal influence on patterns of sales and production. The formation of modern _____ was intimately bound up with the emergence of new forms of monopoly capitalism around the end of the 19th and beginning of the 20th century as one element in corporate strategies to create, organize and where possible control markets, especially for mass produced consumer goods.

a. ACNielsen
b. AMAX
c. ADTECH
d. Advertising

10. _____ is an advertisement in which a particular product specifically mentions a competitor by name for the express purpose of showing why the competitor is inferior to the product naming it.

This should not be confused with parody advertisements, where a fictional product is being advertised for the purpose of poking fun at the particular advertisement, nor should it be confused with the use of a coined brand name for the purpose of comparing the product without actually naming an actual competitor. ('Wikipedia tastes better and is less filling than the Encyclopedia Galactica.')

In the 1980s, during what has been referred to as the cola wars, soft-drink manufacturer Pepsi ran a series of advertisements where people, caught on hidden camera, in a blind taste test, chose Pepsi over rival Coca-Cola.

a. Heavy-up
b. GL-70
c. Cost per conversion
d. Comparative advertising

11. A personal and cultural _____ is a relative ethic _____, an assumption upon which implementation can be extrapolated. A _____ system is a set of consistent _____s and measures that is soo not true. A principle _____ is a foundation upon which other _____s and measures of integrity are based.
a. Package-on-Package
b. Value
c. Supreme Court of the United States
d. Perceptual maps

12. Switching barriers or _____s are terms used in microeconomics, strategic management, and marketing to describe any impediment to a customer's changing of suppliers.

In many markets, consumers are forced to incur costs when switching from one supplier to another. These costs are called _____s and can come in many different shapes.

a. Strategic business unit
b. Switching cost
c. Chaotics
d. Strategic group

13. Why do retail stores need _____? With respect to the key objectives of growth and profit for any retail entity, _____ should significantly improve sales margins and increase sales by enabling the vendor to price variably and hence suitably and to control its product range based on profit margins. The retail stores will be able to compete more effectively with rivals in the form of mixed multiples, mail order and online retailers, who are often able to undercut but who do not generally have the same understanding of the retail market. In particular _____ is recognised as encouraging impulse buys, cross-selling of products and repeat sales.
   a. Power III
   b. 180SearchAssistant
   c. 6-3-5 Brainwriting
   d. Dynamic pricing

14. _____. People may not recognize the value in offered personalization, such as when firms offer to customize product offers. Many people don't want to receive any such offers, period.
   a. Bottling lines
   b. Category Development Index
   c. Push
   d. Little value placed on potential benefits

15. _____ is the process of understanding, anticipating and influencing consumer behavior in order to maximize revenue or profits from a fixed, perishable resource This process was first discovered by Dr. Matt H. Keller. The challenge is to sell the right resources to the right customer at the right time for the right price. This process can result in price discrimination, where a firm charges customers consuming otherwise identical goods or services a different price for doing so.
   a. Multi-level marketing
   b. Yield management
   c. Cross-selling
   d. Service provider

16. _____ is a broad label that refers to any individuals or households that use goods and services generated within the economy. The concept of a _____ is used in different contexts, so that the usage and significance of the term may vary.

A _____ is a person who uses any product or service.

a. Power III
b. 180SearchAssistant
c. 6-3-5 Brainwriting
d. Consumer

17. In marketing a _____ is a ticket or document that can be exchanged for a financial discount or rebate when purchasing a product. Customarily, _____s are issued by manufacturers of consumer packaged goods or by retailers, to be used in retail stores as a part of sales promotions. They are often widely distributed through mail, magazines, newspapers, the Internet, and mobile devices such as cell phones.
   a. Merchandising
   b. Coupon
   c. Marketing communication
   d. Merchandise

18. _____ is a concept that denotes the precise probability of specific eventualities. Technically, the notion of _____ is independent from the notion of value and, as such, eventualities may have both beneficial and adverse consequences. However, in general usage the convention is to focus only on potential negative impact to some characteristic of value that may arise from a future event.
   a. 6-3-5 Brainwriting
   b. Power III
   c. Risk
   d. 180SearchAssistant

19. In economics, _____ describes the state of a market with respect to competition.

   - Perfect competition, in which the market consists of a very large number of firms producing a homogeneous product.
   - Monopolistic competition where there are a large number of independent firms which have a very small proportion of the market share.
   - Oligopoly, in which a market is dominated by a small number of firms which own more than 40% of the market share.
   - Oligopsony, a market dominated by many sellers and a few buyers.
   - Monopoly, where there is only one provider of a product or service.
   - Natural monopoly, a monopoly in which economies of scale cause efficiency to increase continuously with the size of the firm. A firm is a natural monopoly if it is able to serve the entire market demand at a lower cost than any combination of two or more smaller, more specialized firms.
   - Monopsony, when there is only one buyer in a market.

The imperfectly competitive structure is quite identical to the realistic market conditions where some monopolistic competitors, monopolists, oligopolists, and duopolists exist and dominate the market conditions. The elements of _____ include the number and size distribution of firms, entry conditions, and the extent of differentiation.

a. Microeconomics
b. Macroeconomics
c. Money
d. Market structure

20. _____ or consumer demand or consumption is also known as personal consumption expenditure. It is the largest part of aggregate demand or effective demand at the macroeconomic level. There are two variants of consumption in the aggregate demand model, including induced consumption and autonomous consumption.

a. Value added
b. Deregulation
c. Power III
d. Consumer spending

21. In economics, _____ is the desire to own something and the ability to pay for it. The term _____ signifies the ability or the willingness to buy a particular commodity at a given point of time .

a. Discretionary spending
b. Market dominance
c. Market system
d. Demand

22. A _____ is the space, actual or metaphorical, in which a market operates. The term is also used in a trademark law context to denote the actual consumer environment, ie. the 'real world' in which products and services are provided and consumed.

a. Power III
b. Marketplace
c. 6-3-5 Brainwriting
d. 180SearchAssistant

Chapter 13. Internet Retailing

1. _____ consists of the sale of goods or merchandise from a fixed location, such as a department store or kiosk in small or individual lots for direct consumption by the purchaser. _____ may include subordinated services, such as delivery. Purchasers may be individuals or businesses.
   a. Charity shop
   b. Retailing
   c. Warehouse store
   d. Thrifting

2. In economics, business, retail, and accounting, a _____ is the value of money that has been used up to produce something, and hence is not available for use anymore. In economics, a _____ is an alternative that is given up as a result of a decision. In business, the _____ may be one of acquisition, in which case the amount of money expended to acquire it is counted as _____.
   a. Fixed costs
   b. Variable cost
   c. Cost
   d. Transaction cost

3. The _____ is an economic indicator that measures the satisfaction of consumers across the U.S. economy. It is produced by the National Quality Research Center (NQRC) at the University of Michigan in Ann Arbor, Michigan.

   The _____ interviews about 80,000 Americans annually and asks about their satisfaction with the goods and services they have consumed.

   a. ADTECH
   b. AMAX
   c. American Customer Satisfaction Index
   d. ACNielsen

4. _____, a business term, is a measure of how products and services supplied by a company meet or surpass customer expectation. It is seen as a key performance indicator within business and is part of the four perspectives of a Balanced Scorecard.

   In a competitive marketplace where businesses compete for customers, _____ is seen as a key differentiator and increasingly has become a key element of business strategy.

   a. Customer Satisfaction
   b. Supplier diversity
   c. Customer base
   d. Psychological pricing

5. _____ is a list for goods and materials held available in stock by a business. It is also used for a list of the contents of a household and for a list for testamentary purposes of the possessions of someone who has died. In accounting _____ is considered an asset.
   a. Ending Inventory
   b. ACNielsen
   c. ADTECH
   d. Inventory

6. The _____ is an equation that equals the cost of goods sold divided by the average inventory. Average inventory equals beginning inventory plus ending inventory divided by 2.

The formula for _____:

$$\text{Inventory Turnover} = \frac{\text{Cost of Goods Sold}}{\text{Average Inventory}}$$

The formula for average inventory:

$$\text{Average Inventory} = \frac{\text{Beginning inventory} + \text{Ending inventory}}{2}$$

A low turnover rate may point to overstocking, obsolescence, or deficiencies in the product line or marketing effort.

   a. AMAX
   b. ADTECH
   c. ACNielsen
   d. Inventory turnover

7. _____ is one of the four Ps of the marketing mix. The other three aspects are product, promotion, and place. It is also a key variable in microeconomic price allocation theory.
   a. Competitor indexing
   b. Relationship based pricing
   c. Price
   d. Pricing

Chapter 13. Internet Retailing

8. _____ in economics and business is the result of an exchange and from that trade we assign a numerical monetary value to a good, service or asset. If I trade 4 apples for an orange, the _____ of an orange is 4 - apples. Inversely, the _____ of an apple is 1/4 oranges.
   a. Price
   b. Discounts and allowances
   c. Contribution margin-based pricing
   d. Pricing

9. _____ is the examining of goods or services from retailers with the intent to purchase at that time. _____ is an activity of selection and/or purchase. In some contexts it is considered a leisure activity as well as an economic one.
   a. Khodebshchik
   b. Hawkers
   c. Discount store
   d. Shopping

10. _____ is anything that is intended to save time, energy or frustration. A _____ store at a petrol station, for example, sells items that have nothing to do with gasoline/petrol, but it saves the consumer from having to go to a grocery store. '_____' is a very relative term and its meaning tends to change over time.
    a. Marketing buzz
    b. MaxDiff
    c. Demographic profile
    d. Convenience

11. _____ is an advertisement in which a particular product specifically mentions a competitor by name for the express purpose of showing why the competitor is inferior to the product naming it.

This should not be confused with parody advertisements, where a fictional product is being advertised for the purpose of poking fun at the particular advertisement, nor should it be confused with the use of a coined brand name for the purpose of comparing the product without actually naming an actual competitor. ('Wikipedia tastes better and is less filling than the Encyclopedia Galactica.')

In the 1980s, during what has been referred to as the cola wars, soft-drink manufacturer Pepsi ran a series of advertisements where people, caught on hidden camera, in a blind taste test, chose Pepsi over rival Coca-Cola.

   a. Heavy-up
   b. GL-70
   c. Cost per conversion
   d. Comparative advertising

Chapter 13. Internet Retailing

12. _____ is a broad label that refers to any individuals or households that use goods and services generated within the economy. The concept of a _____ is used in different contexts, so that the usage and significance of the term may vary.

A _____ is a person who uses any product or service.

   a. Power III
   b. 6-3-5 Brainwriting
   c. 180SearchAssistant
   d. Consumer

13. A _____ is a statement or claim that a particular event will occur in the future in more certain terms than a forecast. The etymology of this word is Latin . In regards to predicting the future Howard H. Stevenson Says, ' _____ is at least two things: Important and hard.' Important, because we have to act, and hard because we have to realize the future we want, and what is the best way to get there.
   a. 6-3-5 Brainwriting
   b. Power III
   c. 180SearchAssistant
   d. Prediction

14. _____. People may not recognize the value in offered personalization, such as when firms offer to customize product offers. Many people don't want to receive any such offers, period.
   a. Bottling lines
   b. Push
   c. Category Development Index
   d. Little value placed on potential benefits

15. In statistics, an _____ is a term in a statistical model added when the effect of two or more variables is not simply additive. Such a term reflects that the effect of one variable depends on the values of one or more other variables.

Thus, for a response Y and two variables x_1 and x_2 an additive model would be:

$$Y = ax_1 + bx_2 + \text{error}$$

In contrast to this,

$$Y = ax_1 + bx_2 + c(x_1 \times x_2) + \text{error,}$$

is an example of a model with an _____ between variables x_1 and x_2 ('error' refers to the random variable whose value by which y differs from the expected value of y.)

a. ACNielsen
b. ADTECH
c. AMAX
d. Interaction

16. _____ is systematic determination of merit, worth, and significance of something or someone using criteria against a set of standards. _____ often is used to characterize and appraise subjects of interest in a wide range of human enterprises, including the arts, criminal justice, foundations and non-profit organizations, government, health care, and other human services.

Depending on the topic of interest, there are professional groups which look to the quality and rigor of the _____ process.

a. AMAX
b. ACNielsen
c. ADTECH
d. Evaluation

17. _____, also referred to as i-marketing, web marketing, online marketing is the marketing of products or services over the Internet.

The Internet has brought many unique benefits to marketing, one of which being lower costs for the distribution of information and media to a global audience. The interactive nature of _____, both in terms of providing instant response and eliciting responses, is a unique quality of the medium.

a. ADTECH
b. AMAX
c. ACNielsen
d. Internet marketing

18. _____ is defined by the American _____ Association as the activity, set of institutions, and processes for creating, communicating, delivering, and exchanging offerings that have value for customers, clients, partners, and society at large. The term developed from the original meaning which referred literally to going to market, as in shopping, or going to a market to sell goods or services.

_____ practice tends to be seen as a creative industry, which includes advertising, distribution and selling.

a. Marketing
b. Product naming
c. Customer acquisition management
d. Marketing myopia

19. _____ involves disseminating information about a product, product line, brand, or company. It is one of the four key aspects of the marketing mix. (The other three elements are product marketing, pricing, and distribution). P>_____ is generally sub-divided into two parts:

- Above the line _____: Promotion in the media (e.g. TV, radio, newspapers, Internet and Mobile Phones) in which the advertiser pays an advertising agency to place the ad
- Below the line _____: All other _____. Much of this is intended to be subtle enough for the consumer to be unaware that _____ is taking place. E.g. sponsorship, product placement, endorsements, sales _____, merchandising, direct mail, personal selling, public relations, trade shows

a. Bottling lines
b. Cashmere Agency
c. Davie Brown Index
d. Promotion

20. _____ - Prices increase as shipping distances increase. This is sometimes done by drawing concentric circles on a map with the plant or warehouse at the center and each circle defining the boundary of a price zone. Instead of using circles, irregularly shaped price boundaries can be drawn that reflect geography, population density, transportation infrastructure, and shipping cost. The term '_____' can also refer to the practice of setting prices that reflect local competitive conditions, i.e., the market forces of supply and demand, rather than actual cost of transportation.

_____, as practiced in the gasoline industry in the United States, is the pricing of gasoline based on a complex and secret weighting of factors, such as the number of competing stations, number of vehicles, average traffic flow, population density, and geographic characteristics. This can result in two branded gas stations only a few miles apart selling gasoline at a price differential of as much as $0.50 per gallon.

a. Safeguard
b. Zone pricing
c. Geographical pricing
d. Countervailing duties

Chapter 14. Consumer Channels

1. _____ is a broad label that refers to any individuals or households that use goods and services generated within the economy. The concept of a _____ is used in different contexts, so that the usage and significance of the term may vary.

A _____ is a person who uses any product or service.

   a. 180SearchAssistant
   b. Power III
   c. 6-3-5 Brainwriting
   d. Consumer

2. An _____ is the manufacturing of a good or service within a category. Although _____ is a broad term for any kind of economic production, in economics and urban planning _____ is a synonym for the secondary sector, which is a type of economic activity involved in the manufacturing of raw materials into goods and products.

There are four key industrial economic sectors: the primary sector, largely raw material extraction industries such as mining and farming; the secondary sector, involving refining, construction, and manufacturing; the tertiary sector, which deals with services (such as law and medicine) and distribution of manufactured goods; and the quaternary sector, a relatively new type of knowledge _____ focusing on technological research, design and development such as computer programming, and biochemistry.

   a. ACNielsen
   b. Industry
   c. AMAX
   d. ADTECH

3. _____ is an advertisement in which a particular product specifically mentions a competitor by name for the express purpose of showing why the competitor is inferior to the product naming it.

This should not be confused with parody advertisements, where a fictional product is being advertised for the purpose of poking fun at the particular advertisement, nor should it be confused with the use of a coined brand name for the purpose of comparing the product without actually naming an actual competitor. ('Wikipedia tastes better and is less filling than the Encyclopedia Galactica.')

In the 1980s, during what has been referred to as the cola wars, soft-drink manufacturer Pepsi ran a series of advertisements where people, caught on hidden camera, in a blind taste test, chose Pepsi over rival Coca-Cola.

a. Heavy-up
b. Comparative advertising
c. Cost per conversion
d. GL-70

4. _____ is anything that is intended to save time, energy or frustration. A _____ store at a petrol station, for example, sells items that have nothing to do with gasoline/petrol, but it saves the consumer from having to go to a grocery store. '_____' is a very relative term and its meaning tends to change over time.

a. Demographic profile
b. Convenience
c. MaxDiff
d. Marketing buzz

5. On an intranet or B2E Enterprise Web portals, personalization is often based on user attributes such as department, functional area, or role. The term _____ in this context refers to the ability of users to modify the page layout or specify what content should be displayed.

There are two categories of personalizations:

1. Rule-based
2. Content-based

Web personalization models include rules-based filtering, based on 'if this, then that' rules processing, and collaborative filtering, which serves relevant material to customers by combining their own personal preferences with the preferences of like-minded others. Collaborative filtering works well for books, music, video, etc.

a. Customization
b. Cashmere Agency
c. Movin'
d. Self branding

6. _____ or personalisation is tailoring a consumer product, electronic or written medium to a user based on personal details or characteristics they provide. More recently, it has especially been applied in the context of the World Wide Web.

Web pages are personalized based on the interests of an individual.

a. Flighting
b. Complex sale
c. Personalization
d. Sexism,

7. _____ in economics and business is the result of an exchange and from that trade we assign a numerical monetary value to a good, service or asset. If I trade 4 apples for an orange, the _____ of an orange is 4 - apples. Inversely, the _____ of an apple is 1/4 oranges.
   a. Discounts and allowances
   b. Price
   c. Contribution margin-based pricing
   d. Pricing

8. A personal and cultural _____ is a relative ethic _____, an assumption upon which implementation can be extrapolated. A _____ system is a set of consistent _____s and measures that is soo not true. A principle _____ is a foundation upon which other _____s and measures of integrity are based.
   a. Value
   b. Package-on-Package
   c. Perceptual maps
   d. Supreme Court of the United States

9. _____ consists of the sale of goods or merchandise from a fixed location, such as a department store or kiosk in small or individual lots for direct consumption by the purchaser. _____ may include subordinated services, such as delivery. Purchasers may be individuals or businesses.
   a. Thrifting
   b. Warehouse store
   c. Charity shop
   d. Retailing

10. Merchandising refers to the methods, practices and operations conducted to promote and sustain certain categories of commercial activity. The term is understood to have different specific meanings depending on the context. _____ is a sale goods at a store

In marketing, one of the definitions of merchandising is the practice in which the brand or image from one product or service is used to sell another.

a. Merchandising
b. Merchandise
c. Sales promotion
d. New Media Strategies

11. _____ is an Internet-based marketing practice in which a business rewards one or more affiliates for each visitor or customer brought about by the affiliate's marketing efforts.

_____ is also the name of the industry where a number of different types of companies and individuals are performing this form of Internet marketing, including affiliate networks, affiliate management companies, and in-house affiliate managers, specialized third party vendors, and various types of affiliates/publishers who promote the products and services of their partners.

_____ overlaps with other Internet marketing methods to some degree, because affiliates often use regular advertising methods.

a. ADTECH
b. AMAX
c. ACNielsen
d. Affiliate marketing

12. _____ is defined by the American _____ Association as the activity, set of institutions, and processes for creating, communicating, delivering, and exchanging offerings that have value for customers, clients, partners, and society at large. The term developed from the original meaning which referred literally to going to market, as in shopping, or going to a market to sell goods or services.

_____ practice tends to be seen as a creative industry, which includes advertising, distribution and selling.

a. Marketing myopia
b. Customer acquisition management
c. Product naming
d. Marketing

13. _____ is one of the four elements of marketing mix. An organization or set of organizations (go-betweens) involved in the process of making a product or service available for use or consumption by a consumer or business user.

The other three parts of the marketing mix are product, pricing, and promotion.

Chapter 14. Consumer Channels 95

a. Distribution
b. Better Living Through Chemistry
c. Japan Advertising Photographers' Association
d. Comparison-Shopping agent

14. A _____ is a type of wholesale merchant business that buys goods and bulk products from importers, other wholesalers and then sells to retailers. _____s can deal in any commodity destined for the retail market. Typical categories are food, lumber, hardware, fuel, and textiles.

a. Jobbing house
b. Refusal to deal
c. Chief privacy officer
d. Tacit collusion

15. _____ is the examining of goods or services from retailers with the intent to purchase at that time. _____ is an activity of selection and/or purchase. In some contexts it is considered a leisure activity as well as an economic one.

a. Khodebshchik
b. Discount store
c. Hawkers
d. Shopping

16. _____ describes the situation when output from (or information about the result of) an event or phenomenon in the past will influence the same event/phenomenon in the present or future. When an event is part of a chain of cause-and-effect that forms a circuit or loop, then the event is said to 'feed back' into itself.

_____ is also a synonym for:

- _____ Signal; the information about the initial event that is the basis for subsequent modification of the event.
- _____ Loop; the causal path that leads from the initial generation of the _____ signal to the subsequent modification of the event.

_____ is a mechanism, process or signal that is looped back to control a system within itself. Such a loop is called a _____ loop.

a. 180SearchAssistant
b. Power III
c. 6-3-5 Brainwriting
d. Feedback

17. In statistics, an _____ is a term in a statistical model added when the effect of two or more variables is not simply additive. Such a term reflects that the effect of one variable depends on the values of one or more other variables.

Thus, for a response Y and two variables x_1 and x_2 an additive model would be:

$$Y = ax_1 + bx_2 + \text{error}$$

In contrast to this,

$$Y = ax_1 + bx_2 + c(x_1 \times x_2) + \text{error},$$

is an example of a model with an _____ between variables x_1 and x_2 ('error' refers to the random variable whose value by which y differs from the expected value of y.)

a. ADTECH
b. AMAX
c. Interaction
d. ACNielsen

18. _____ occurs when manufacturers (brands) disintermediate their channel partners, such as distributors, retailers, dealers, and sales representatives, by selling their products direct to consumers through general marketing methods and/or over the internet through eCommerce.

Some manufacturers want their brands to capture the power of the internet but do not want to create conflict with their other distribution channels, as these partners are necessary and viable for any manufacturer to maintain and gain success. The Census Bureau of the U.S. Department of Commerce reported that online sales in 2005 grew 24.6 percent over 2004 to reach 86.3 billion dollars.

a. Trade Symbols
b. Retail design
c. Store brand
d. Channel conflict

19. _____ is one of the four Ps of the marketing mix. The other three aspects are product, promotion, and place. It is also a key variable in microeconomic price allocation theory.

a. Relationship based pricing
b. Competitor indexing
c. Price
d. Pricing

20. _____ refer to a collection of facts usually collected as the result of experience, observation or experiment or a set of premises. This may consist of numbers, words particularly as measurements or observations of a set of variables. _____ are often viewed as a lowest level of abstraction from which information and knowledge are derived.
   a. Sample size
   b. Mean
   c. Pearson product-moment correlation coefficient
   d. Data

21. The _____ is an economic and political union of 27 member states, located primarily in Europe. It was established by the Treaty of Maastricht on 1 November 1993 upon the foundations of the pre-existing European Economic Community. With almost 500 million citizens, the _____ combined generates an estimated 30% share (US$16.8 trillion in 2007) of the nominal gross world product.
   a. Eurozone
   b. ADTECH
   c. ACNielsen
   d. European Union

22. A _____ is an entity that provides services to other entities. Usually this refers to a business that provides subscription or web service to other businesses or individuals. Examples of these services include Internet access, Mobile phone operator, and web application hosting.
   a. Cross-selling
   b. Yield management
   c. Freebie marketing
   d. Service provider

23. A _____ or clearance is the final sale of an item or items to zero inventory. It may be a given model of item that is not selling well, or in the case of the final closure of a retailer because of a relocation, a fire (fire sale), or especially because of a bankruptcy. In the latter case, it is usually known as a going-out-of-business sale, and is part of a liquidation.

Chapter 14. Consumer Channels

a. Warehouse store
b. Bulk bins
c. Khodebshchik
d. Closeout

24. An _____ or factory outlet or 'Best Saving Outlet' is a retail store in which manufacturers sell their stock directly to the public through their own branded stores. The stores can be brick and mortar or online. Traditionally, a factory outlet was a store, attached to a factory or warehouse.
   a. Electronic Shelf Label
   b. Endcap
   c. Online ticket brokering
   d. Outlet store

25. _____ was a writer, management consultant, and self-described 'social ecologist.' Widely considered to be the father of 'modern management,' his 39 books and countless scholarly and popular articles explored how humans are organized across all sectors of society--in business, government and the nonprofit world. His writings have predicted many of the major developments of the late twentieth century, including privatization and decentralization; the rise of Japan to economic world power; the decisive importance of marketing; and the emergence of the information society with its necessity of lifelong learning. In 1959, Drucker coined the term 'knowledge worker' and later in his life considered knowledge work productivity to be the next frontier of management.
   a. Peter Ferdinand Drucker
   b. Paschal Eze
   c. Rick Boyce
   d. Nouveau riche

26. In economics, business, retail, and accounting, a _____ is the value of money that has been used up to produce something, and hence is not available for use anymore. In economics, a _____ is an alternative that is given up as a result of a decision. In business, the _____ may be one of acquisition, in which case the amount of money expended to acquire it is counted as _____.
   a. Cost
   b. Transaction cost
   c. Variable cost
   d. Fixed costs

27. A _____ is a framework for creating economic, social, and/or other forms of value. The term _____ is thus used for a broad range of informal and formal descriptions to represent core aspects of a business, including purpose, offerings, strategies, infrastructure, organizational structures, trading practices, and operational processes and policies.

In the most basic sense, a _____ is the method of doing business by which a company can sustain itself -- that is, generate revenue.

a. Yield management
b. Business model
c. Service provider
d. Pay to surf

Chapter 15. B2B e-Commerce

1. _____ is the suppression of speech or deletion of communicative material which may be considered objectionable, harmful, sensitive, or inconvenient to the government or media organizations as determined by a censor.

The rationale for _____ is different for various types of information censored:

- Moral _____, is the removal of materials that are obscene or otherwise morally questionable. Pornography, for example, is often censored under this rationale, especially child pornography, which is censored in most jurisdictions in the world.
- Military _____ is the process of keeping military intelligence and tactics confidential and away from the enemy. This is used to counter espionage, which is the process of gleaning military information. Very often, militaries will also attempt to suppress politically inconvenient information even if that information has no actual intelligence value.
- Political _____ occurs when governments hold back information from their citizens. The logic is to exert control over the populace and prevent free expression that might foment rebellion.
- Religious _____ is the means by which any material objectionable to a certain faith is removed. This often involves a dominant religion forcing limitations on less prevalent ones. Alternatively, one religion may shun the works of another when they believe the content is not appropriate for their faith.
- Corporate _____ is the process by which editors in corporate media outlets intervene to halt the publishing of information that portrays their business or business partners in a negative light.

Strict _____ existed in the Eastern Bloc. Throughout the bloc, the various ministries of culture held a tight reign on their writers. Cultural products there reflected the propaganda needs of the state.

a. 6-3-5 Brainwriting
b. 180SearchAssistant
c. Power III
d. Censorship

2. A _____ is a type of wholesale merchant business that buys goods and bulk products from importers, other wholesalers and then sells to retailers. _____s can deal in any commodity destined for the retail market. Typical categories are food, lumber, hardware, fuel, and textiles.
a. Jobbing house
b. Tacit collusion
c. Chief privacy officer
d. Refusal to deal

3. A _____ or logistics network is the system of organizations, people, technology, activities, information and resources involved in moving a product or service from supplier to customer. _____ activities transform natural resources, raw materials and components into a finished product that is delivered to the end customer. In sophisticated _____ systems, used products may re-enter the _____ at any point where residual value is recyclable.

a. Demand chain management
b. Purchasing
c. Supply chain network
d. Supply chain

4. _____ refers to the structured transmission of data between organizations by electronic means. It is used to transfer electronic documents from one computer system to another (ie) from one trading partner to another trading partner. It is more than mere E-mail; for instance, organizations might replace bills of lading and even checks with appropriate _____ messages.
   a. ADTECH
   b. Electronic data interchange
   c. AMAX
   d. ACNielsen

5. _____ refer to a collection of facts usually collected as the result of experience, observation or experiment or a set of premises. This may consist of numbers, words particularly as measurements or observations of a set of variables. _____ are often viewed as a lowest level of abstraction from which information and knowledge are derived.
   a. Sample size
   b. Mean
   c. Pearson product-moment correlation coefficient
   d. Data

6. A _____, in marketing, procurement, and organizational studies, is a group of employees, family members, or members of any type of organization responsible for purchasing an item for the organization. In a business setting, major purchases typically require input from various parts of the organization, including finance, accounting, purchasing, information technology management, and senior management. Highly technical purchases, such as information systems or production equipment, also require the expertise of technical specialists.
   a. Buying center
   b. Marketing myopia
   c. Commercialization
   d. Packshot

7. _____ is one of the four elements of marketing mix. An organization or set of organizations (go-betweens) involved in the process of making a product or service available for use or consumption by a consumer or business user.

The other three parts of the marketing mix are product, pricing, and promotion.

a. Better Living Through Chemistry
b. Japan Advertising Photographers' Association
c. Comparison-Shopping agent
d. Distribution

8. _____ is subcontracting a process, such as product design or manufacturing, to a third-party company. The decision to outsource is often made in the interest of lowering cost or making better use of time and energy costs, redirecting or conserving energy directed at the competencies of a particular business, or to make more efficient use of land, labor, capital, (information) technology and resources. _____ became part of the business lexicon during the 1980s.

a. Outsourcing
b. Intangible assets
c. In-house
d. ACNielsen

9. _____ is an advertisement in which a particular product specifically mentions a competitor by name for the express purpose of showing why the competitor is inferior to the product naming it.

This should not be confused with parody advertisements, where a fictional product is being advertised for the purpose of poking fun at the particular advertisement, nor should it be confused with the use of a coined brand name for the purpose of comparing the product without actually naming an actual competitor. ('Wikipedia tastes better and is less filling than the Encyclopedia Galactica.')

In the 1980s, during what has been referred to as the cola wars, soft-drink manufacturer Pepsi ran a series of advertisements where people, caught on hidden camera, in a blind taste test, chose Pepsi over rival Coca-Cola.

a. Cost per conversion
b. GL-70
c. Heavy-up
d. Comparative advertising

10. An _____ is the manufacturing of a good or service within a category. Although _____ is a broad term for any kind of economic production, in economics and urban planning _____ is a synonym for the secondary sector, which is a type of economic activity involved in the manufacturing of raw materials into goods and products.

There are four key industrial economic sectors: the primary sector, largely raw material extraction industries such as mining and farming; the secondary sector, involving refining, construction, and manufacturing; the tertiary sector, which deals with services (such as law and medicine) and distribution of manufactured goods; and the quaternary sector, a relatively new type of knowledge _____ focusing on technological research, design and development such as computer programming, and biochemistry.

a. AMAX
b. ADTECH
c. ACNielsen
d. Industry

11. _____ is a term commonly used to describe commerce transactions between businesses like the one between a manufacturer and a wholesaler or a wholesaler and a retailer i.e both the buyer and the seller are business entity.This is unlike business-to-consumers (B2C) which involve a business entity and end consumer, or business-to-government (B2G) which involve a business entity and government.

The volume of B2B transactions is much higher than the volume of B2C transactions. The primary reason for this is that in a typical supply chain there will be many B2B transactions involving subcomponent or raw materials, and only one B2C transaction, specifically sale of the finished product to the end customer.

a. Business-to-business
b. Customer relationship management
c. Social marketing
d. Disruptive technology

12. A _____ is the space, actual or metaphorical, in which a market operates. The term is also used in a trademark law context to denote the actual consumer environment, ie. the 'real world' in which products and services are provided and consumed.
a. 6-3-5 Brainwriting
b. Power III
c. Marketplace
d. 180SearchAssistant

13. In economics, _____ describes the state of a market with respect to competition.

- Perfect competition, in which the market consists of a very large number of firms producing a homogeneous product.
- Monopolistic competition where there are a large number of independent firms which have a very small proportion of the market share.
- Oligopoly, in which a market is dominated by a small number of firms which own more than 40% of the market share.
- Oligopsony, a market dominated by many sellers and a few buyers.
- Monopoly, where there is only one provider of a product or service.
- Natural monopoly, a monopoly in which economies of scale cause efficiency to increase continuously with the size of the firm. A firm is a natural monopoly if it is able to serve the entire market demand at a lower cost than any combination of two or more smaller, more specialized firms.
- Monopsony, when there is only one buyer in a market.

The imperfectly competitive structure is quite identical to the realistic market conditions where some monopolistic competitors, monopolists, oligopolists, and duopolists exist and dominate the market conditions. The elements of _____ include the number and size distribution of firms, entry conditions, and the extent of differentiation.

a. Microeconomics
b. Money
c. Macroeconomics
d. Market structure

14. The _____ is an observed phenomenon in forecast-driven distribution channels. The concept has its roots in J Forrester's Industrial Dynamics (1961) and thus it is also known as the Forrester Effect. Since the oscillating demand magnification upstream a supply chain reminds someone of a cracking whip it became famous as the _____.
a. Nielsen VideoScan
b. Free box
c. Bullwhip effect
d. Wholesale list

15. In economics, _____ is the desire to own something and the ability to pay for it. The term _____ signifies the ability or the willingness to buy a particular commodity at a given point of time .

a. Discretionary spending
b. Market system
c. Market dominance
d. Demand

16. _____ is a list for goods and materials held available in stock by a business. It is also used for a list of the contents of a household and for a list for testamentary purposes of the possessions of someone who has died. In accounting _____ is considered an asset.
a. Ending Inventory
b. ACNielsen
c. Inventory
d. ADTECH

Chapter 15. B2B e-Commerce

17. _____ is a family of business models in which the buyer of a product provides certain information to a supplier of that product and the supplier takes full responsibility for maintaining an agreed inventory of the material, usually at the buyer's consumption location (usually a store.) A third party logistics provider can also be involved to make sure that the buyer have the required level of inventory by adjusting the demand and supply gaps.

As a symbiotic relationship, _____ makes it less likely that a business will unintentionally become out of stock of a good and reduces inventory in the supply chain.

   a. Customer driven supply chain
   b. Merchandise management system
   c. Reverse auction
   d. Vendor managed inventory

18. In economics, business, retail, and accounting, a _____ is the value of money that has been used up to produce something, and hence is not available for use anymore. In economics, a _____ is an alternative that is given up as a result of a decision. In business, the _____ may be one of acquisition, in which case the amount of money expended to acquire it is counted as _____.
   a. Fixed costs
   b. Transaction cost
   c. Cost
   d. Variable cost

19. In business and engineering, _____ is the term used to describe the complete process of bringing a new product or service to market. There are two parallel paths involved in the _____ process: one involves the idea generation, product design, and detail engineering; the other involves market research and marketing analysis. Companies typically see _____ as the first stage in generating and commercializing new products within the overall strategic process of product life cycle management used to maintain or grow their market share.
   a. New product development
   b. Product development
   c. Product optimization
   d. Specification

20. In business and engineering, new _____ is the term used to describe the complete process of bringing a new product or service to market. There are two parallel paths involved in the Nproduct development process: one involves the idea generation, product design, and detail engineering; the other involves market research and marketing analysis. Companies typically see new _____ as the first stage in generating and commercializing new products within the overall strategic process of product life cycle management used to maintain or grow their market share.

a. New product development
b. New product screening
c. Specification tree
d. Product development

Chapter 16. Online Research

1. _____ are used to collect quantitative information about items in a population. Surveys of human populations and institutions are common in political polling and government, health, social science and marketing research. A survey may focus on opinions or factual information depending on its purpose, and many surveys involve administering questions to individuals.
   a. Gross Margin Return on Inventory Investment
   b. Convergent
   c. BeyondROI
   d. Statistical surveys

2. _____ is a way of expressing knowledge or belief that an event will occur or has occurred. In mathematics the concept has been given an exact meaning in _____ theory, that is used extensively in such areas of study as mathematics, statistics, finance, gambling, science, and philosophy to draw conclusions about the likelihood of potential events and the underlying mechanics of complex systems.
   a. Data
   b. Linear regression
   c. Heteroskedastic
   d. Probability

3. _____ is that part of statistical practice concerned with the selection of individual observations intended to yield some knowledge about a population of concern, especially for the purposes of statistical inference. Each observation measures one or more properties (weight, location, etc.) of an observable entity enumerated to distinguish objects or individuals.
   a. Richard Buckminster 'Bucky' Fuller
   b. Sampling
   c. AStore
   d. Sports Marketing Group

4. _____ is anything that is intended to save time, energy or frustration. A _____ store at a petrol station, for example, sells items that have nothing to do with gasoline/petrol, but it saves the consumer from having to go to a grocery store. '_____' is a very relative term and its meaning tends to change over time.
   a. Marketing buzz
   b. Demographic profile
   c. MaxDiff
   d. Convenience

5. An _____ is a survey of public opinion from a particular sample. _____s are usually designed to represent the opinions of a population by conducting a series of questions and then extrapolating generalities in ratio or within confidence intervals.

Chapter 16. Online Research

The first known example of an _____ was a local straw poll conducted by The Harrisburg Pennsylvanian in 1824, showing Andrew Jackson leading John Quincy Adams by 335 votes to 169 in the contest for the United States Presidency.

a. ADTECH
b. ACNielsen
c. AMAX
d. Opinion poll

6. _____ is the difference between a measured value of quantity and its true value. In statistics, an error is not a 'mistake'. Variability is an inherent part of things being measured and of the measurement process.

a. AMAX
b. ACNielsen
c. ADTECH
d. Observational error

7. _____ in survey research refers to the ratio of number of people who answered the survey divided by the number of people in the sample. It is usually expressed in the form of a percentage.

Example: if 1,000 surveys were sent by mail, and 257 were successfully completed and returned, then the _____ would be 25.7 %.

a. Reference value
b. Response rate
c. Sentence completion tests
d. Power III

8. _____ is a standard point of view or personal prejudice. especially when the tendency interferes with the ability to be impartial, unprejudiced, or objective. The term _____ed is used to describe an action, judgment, or other outcome influenced by a prejudged perspective.

a. 6-3-5 Brainwriting
b. Bias
c. Power III
d. 180SearchAssistant

9. _____ often refers to either primary or secondary research. Secondary research involves a company using information compiled from various sources, which is about a new or existing product. The advantages of secondary research are that it is relatively cheap and easily accessible.

   a. Mystery shopping
   b. Mystery shoppers
   c. Questionnaire
   d. Market research

10. A _____ is a collection of symbols, experiences and associations connected with a product, a service, a person or any other artifact or entity.

    _____s have become increasingly important components of culture and the economy, now being described as 'cultural accessories and personal philosophies'.

    Some people distinguish the psychological aspect of a _____ from the experiential aspect.

    a. Brand equity
    b. Brandable software
    c. Store brand
    d. Brand

11. _____ is the structure of brands within an organizational entity. It is the way in which the brands within a company's portfolio are related to, and differentiated from, one another. The architecture should define the different leagues of branding within the organization; how the corporate brand and sub-brands relate to and support each other; and how the sub-brands reflect or reinforce the core purpose of the corporate brand to which they belong.

    a. Corporate colours
    b. Channel conflict
    c. Brand architecture
    d. Status brand

12. _____ refer to a collection of facts usually collected as the result of experience, observation or experiment or a set of premises. This may consist of numbers, words particularly as measurements or observations of a set of variables. _____ are often viewed as a lowest level of abstraction from which information and knowledge are derived.

    a. Mean
    b. Pearson product-moment correlation coefficient
    c. Sample size
    d. Data

13. _____ consists of the sale of goods or merchandise from a fixed location, such as a department store or kiosk in small or individual lots for direct consumption by the purchaser. _____ may include subordinated services, such as delivery. Purchasers may be individuals or businesses.
    a. Charity shop
    b. Retailing
    c. Warehouse store
    d. Thrifting

14. _____ or _____ data refers to selected population characteristics as used in government, marketing or opinion research, or the _____ profiles used in such research. Note the distinction from the term 'demography' Commonly-used _____ include race, age, income, disabilities, mobility (in terms of travel time to work or number of vehicles available), educational attainment, home ownership, employment status, and even location.
    a. AStore
    b. African Americans
    c. Albert Einstein
    d. Demographic

15. In environmental modeling and especially in hydrology, a _____ model means a model that is acceptably consistent with observed natural processes, i.e. that simulates well, for example, observed river discharge. It is a key concept of the so-called Generalized Likelihood Uncertainty Estimation (GLUE) methodology to quantify how uncertain environmental predictions are.
    a. Behavioral
    b. Power III
    c. 6-3-5 Brainwriting
    d. 180SearchAssistant

16. In marketing and advertising, a _____ usually an advertising campaign, is aimed at appealing to. A _____ can be people of a certain age group, gender, marital status, etc. (ex: teenagers, females, single people, etc.)
    a. National brand
    b. Targeted advertising
    c. Brand Development Index
    d. Target audience

17. Competitiveness is a comparative concept of the ability and performance of a firm, sub-sector or country to sell and supply goods and/or services in a given market. Although widely used in economics and business management, the usefulness of the concept, particularly in the context of national competitiveness, is vigorously disputed by economists, such as Paul Krugman .

The term may also be applied to markets, where it is used to refer to the extent to which the market structure may be regarded as perfectly _____.

a. Customs union
b. Free trade zone
c. Competitive
d. Geographical pricing

18. _____ is, in very basic words, a position a firm occupies against its competitors.

According to Michael Porter, the three methods for creating a sustainable _____ are through:

1. Cost leadership - Cost advantage occurs when a firm delivers the same services as its competitors but at a lower cost;

2.

a. Power III
b. 180SearchAssistant
c. 6-3-5 Brainwriting
d. Competitive advantage

19. In economics, business, retail, and accounting, a _____ is the value of money that has been used up to produce something, and hence is not available for use anymore. In economics, a _____ is an alternative that is given up as a result of a decision. In business, the _____ may be one of acquisition, in which case the amount of money expended to acquire it is counted as _____.

a. Variable cost
b. Fixed costs
c. Transaction cost
d. Cost

20. _____ is an advertisement in which a particular product specifically mentions a competitor by name for the express purpose of showing why the competitor is inferior to the product naming it.

This should not be confused with parody advertisements, where a fictional product is being advertised for the purpose of poking fun at the particular advertisement, nor should it be confused with the use of a coined brand name for the purpose of comparing the product without actually naming an actual competitor. ('Wikipedia tastes better and is less filling than the Encyclopedia Galactica.')

In the 1980s, during what has been referred to as the cola wars, soft-drink manufacturer Pepsi ran a series of advertisements where people, caught on hidden camera, in a blind taste test, chose Pepsi over rival Coca-Cola.

a. Heavy-up
b. Comparative advertising
c. GL-70
d. Cost per conversion

21. In psychology, philosophy, and the cognitive sciences, _____ is the process of attaining awareness or understanding of sensory information. It is a task far more complex than was imagined in the 1950s and 1960s, when it was predicted that building perceiving machines would take about a decade, a goal which is still very far from fruition. The word _____ comes from the Latin words _____, percepio, meaning 'receiving, collecting, action of taking possession, apprehension with the mind or senses.'

_____ is one of the oldest fields in psychology.

a. Groupthink
b. Perception
c. 180SearchAssistant
d. Power III

Chapter 17. Organizing for Online Marketing

1. On an intranet or B2E Enterprise Web portals, personalization is often based on user attributes such as department, functional area, or role. The term _____ in this context refers to the ability of users to modify the page layout or specify what content should be displayed.

There are two categories of personalizations:

1. Rule-based
2. Content-based

Web personalization models include rules-based filtering, based on 'if this, then that' rules processing, and collaborative filtering, which serves relevant material to customers by combining their own personal preferences with the preferences of like-minded others. Collaborative filtering works well for books, music, video, etc.

a. Customization
b. Self branding
c. Cashmere Agency
d. Movin'

2. In statistics, an _____ is a term in a statistical model added when the effect of two or more variables is not simply additive. Such a term reflects that the effect of one variable depends on the values of one or more other variables.

Thus, for a response Y and two variables x_1 and x_2 an additive model would be:

$$Y = ax_1 + bx_2 + \text{error}$$

In contrast to this,

$$Y = ax_1 + bx_2 + c(x_1 \times x_2) + \text{error},$$

is an example of a model with an _____ between variables x_1 and x_2 ('error' refers to the random variable whose value by which y differs from the expected value of y.)

a. Interaction
b. AMAX
c. ACNielsen
d. ADTECH

3. _____ or personalisation is tailoring a consumer product, electronic or written medium to a user based on personal details or characteristics they provide. More recently, it has especially been applied in the context of the World Wide Web.

Web pages are personalized based on the interests of an individual.

   a. Complex sale
   b. Personalization
   c. Flighting
   d. Sexism,

4. A _____ is a plan of action designed to achieve a particular goal.

   _____ is different from tactics. In military terms, tactics is concerned with the conduct of an engagement while _____ is concerned with how different engagements are linked.

   a. 6-3-5 Brainwriting
   b. Power III
   c. Strategy
   d. 180SearchAssistant

5. A personal and cultural _____ is a relative ethic _____, an assumption upon which implementation can be extrapolated. A _____ system is a set of consistent _____s and measures that is soo not true. A principle _____ is a foundation upon which other _____s and measures of integrity are based.

   a. Value
   b. Perceptual maps
   c. Supreme Court of the United States
   d. Package-on-Package

6. _____ is a broad label that refers to any individuals or households that use goods and services generated within the economy. The concept of a _____ is used in different contexts, so that the usage and significance of the term may vary.

   A _____ is a person who uses any product or service.

   a. Power III
   b. Consumer
   c. 180SearchAssistant
   d. 6-3-5 Brainwriting

Chapter 17. Organizing for Online Marketing

7. _____ is an organizational lifecycle function within a company dealing with the planning or marketing of a product or products at all stages of the product lifecycle.

_____ and product marketing (outbound focused) are different yet complementary efforts with the objective of maximizing sales revenues, market share, and profit margins. The role of _____ spans many activities from strategic to tactical and varies based on the organizational structure of the company.

   a. Service product management
   b. Product information management
   c. Requirement prioritization
   d. Product management

8. A _____ researches, selects, develops, and places a company's products.

A _____ considers numerous factors such as target demographic, the products offered by the competition, and how well the product fits in with the company's business model. Generally, a _____ manages one or more tangible products.

   a. Promotional mix
   b. Pick and pack
   c. Power III
   d. Product manager

9. _____ is one of the four elements of marketing mix. An organization or set of organizations (go-betweens) involved in the process of making a product or service available for use or consumption by a consumer or business user.

The other three parts of the marketing mix are product, pricing, and promotion.

   a. Japan Advertising Photographers' Association
   b. Comparison-Shopping agent
   c. Better Living Through Chemistry
   d. Distribution

10. An _____ is the manufacturing of a good or service within a category. Although _____ is a broad term for any kind of economic production, in economics and urban planning _____ is a synonym for the secondary sector, which is a type of economic activity involved in the manufacturing of raw materials into goods and products.

There are four key industrial economic sectors: the primary sector, largely raw material extraction industries such as mining and farming; the secondary sector, involving refining, construction, and manufacturing; the tertiary sector, which deals with services (such as law and medicine) and distribution of manufactured goods; and the quaternary sector, a relatively new type of knowledge _____ focusing on technological research, design and development such as computer programming, and biochemistry.

   a. ADTECH
   b. ACNielsen
   c. AMAX
   d. Industry

11. _____ is a form of intellectual property which gives the creator of an original work exclusive rights for a certain time period in relation to that work, including its publication, distribution and adaptation; after which time the work is said to enter the public domain. _____ applies to any expressible form of an idea or information that is substantive and discrete. Some jurisdictions also recognize 'moral rights' of the creator of a work, such as the right to be credited for the work.
   a. Celler-Kefauver Act
   b. Copyright
   c. Collective mark
   d. Reasonable person standard

12. _____ are legal property rights over creations of the mind, both artistic and commercial, and the corresponding fields of law. Under _____ law, owners are granted certain exclusive rights to a variety of intangible assets, such as musical, literary, and artistic works; ideas, discoveries and inventions; and words, phrases, symbols, and designs. Common types of _____ include copyrights, trademarks, patents, industrial design rights and trade secrets.
   a. Elasticity
   b. ACNielsen
   c. Opinion leadership
   d. Intellectual property

13. A _____ is a collection of symbols, experiences and associations connected with a product, a service, a person or any other artifact or entity.

_____s have become increasingly important components of culture and the economy, now being described as 'cultural accessories and personal philosophies'.

Some people distinguish the psychological aspect of a _____ from the experiential aspect.

a. Brand
b. Store brand
c. Brandable software
d. Brand equity

14. _____ is the structure of brands within an organizational entity. It is the way in which the brands within a company's portfolio are related to, and differentiated from, one another. The architecture should define the different leagues of branding within the organization; how the corporate brand and sub-brands relate to and support each other; and how the sub-brands reflect or reinforce the core purpose of the corporate brand to which they belong.
    a. Status brand
    b. Brand architecture
    c. Corporate colours
    d. Channel conflict

15. _____ is the study of the Earth and its lands, features, inhabitants, and phenomena. A literal translation would be 'to describe or write about the Earth'. The first person to use the word '_____' was Eratosthenes .
    a. Power III
    b. 6-3-5 Brainwriting
    c. Geography
    d. 180SearchAssistant

16. The _____ is an independent agency of the United States government, established in 1914 by the _____ Act. Its principal mission is the promotion of 'consumer protection' and the elimination and prevention of what regulators perceive to be harmfully 'anti-competitive' business practices, such as coercive monopoly.

    The _____ Act was one of President Wilson's major acts against trusts.

    a. 6-3-5 Brainwriting
    b. 180SearchAssistant
    c. Federal Trade Commission
    d. Power III

17. _____ refer to a collection of facts usually collected as the result of experience, observation or experiment or a set of premises. This may consist of numbers, words particularly as measurements or observations of a set of variables. _____ are often viewed as a lowest level of abstraction from which information and knowledge are derived.

Chapter 17. Organizing for Online Marketing

   a. Mean
   b. Data
   c. Sample size
   d. Pearson product-moment correlation coefficient

18. The _____ is an American federal law (codified at 15 U.S.C. § 1681 et seq.) that regulates the collection, dissemination, and use of consumer credit information.
   a. Power III
   b. 6-3-5 Brainwriting
   c. 180SearchAssistant
   d. Fair Credit Reporting Act

19. _____ is the ability of an individual or group to seclude themselves or information about themselves and thereby reveal themselves selectively. The boundaries and content of what is considered private differ among cultures and individuals, but share basic common themes. _____ is sometimes related to anonymity, the wish to remain unnoticed or unidentified in the public realm.
   a. 180SearchAssistant
   b. 6-3-5 Brainwriting
   c. Power III
   d. Privacy

20. In law, _____ also called calumny, libel for written words, slander for spoken words, is the communication of a statement that makes a claim, expressly stated or implied to be factual, that may give an individual, business, product, group, government or nation a negative image. It is usually, but not always, a requirement that this claim be false and that the publication is communicated to someone other than the person defamed

In common law jurisdictions, slander refers to a malicious, false and defamatory spoken statement or report, while libel refers to any other form of communication such as written words or images.

   a. Free good
   b. Muckraker
   c. Free trade zone
   d. Defamation

21. _____, also referred to as i-marketing, web marketing, online marketing is the marketing of products or services over the Internet.

The Internet has brought many unique benefits to marketing, one of which being lower costs for the distribution of information and media to a global audience. The interactive nature of _____, both in terms of providing instant response and eliciting responses, is a unique quality of the medium.

a. AMAX
b. ACNielsen
c. ADTECH
d. Internet marketing

22. _____ is defined by the American _____ Association as the activity, set of institutions, and processes for creating, communicating, delivering, and exchanging offerings that have value for customers, clients, partners, and society at large. The term developed from the original meaning which referred literally to going to market, as in shopping, or going to a market to sell goods or services.

_____ practice tends to be seen as a creative industry, which includes advertising, distribution and selling.

a. Customer acquisition management
b. Marketing myopia
c. Product naming
d. Marketing

23. _____ consists of the sale of goods or merchandise from a fixed location, such as a department store or kiosk in small or individual lots for direct consumption by the purchaser. _____ may include subordinated services, such as delivery. Purchasers may be individuals or businesses.

a. Warehouse store
b. Charity shop
c. Thrifting
d. Retailing

Chapter 1

1. c	2. b	3. b	4. d	5. c	6. d	7. c	8. c	9. d	10. d
11. b	12. d	13. d	14. a	15. d	16. a	17. c	18. d	19. d	20. d
21. b	22. d	23. c	24. c	25. b	26. c	27. c	28. d	29. d	30. d
31. d	32. a	33. c	34. d						

Chapter 2

1. b	2. d	3. d	4. d	5. a	6. c	7. d	8. d	9. d	10. b
11. d	12. a	13. a	14. c	15. c	16. d				

Chapter 3

1. c	2. d	3. d	4. d	5. d	6. d	7. d	8. d	9. d	10. d
11. a	12. d	13. d	14. c	15. d	16. b	17. d	18. b	19. d	20. a
21. b	22. c								

Chapter 4

1. d	2. b	3. d	4. d	5. a	6. d	7. b	8. a	9. d	10. b
11. c	12. a	13. d	14. a	15. d	16. c	17. d	18. d	19. c	20. d

Chapter 5

1. d	2. a	3. d	4. d	5. d	6. d	7. d	8. c	9. d	10. d
11. b	12. d	13. a	14. a	15. a	16. d	17. d	18. b	19. c	20. d
21. a	22. a	23. c							

Chapter 6

1. c	2. b	3. d	4. c	5. a	6. d	7. d	8. c	9. c	10. d
11. d	12. c	13. b	14. a	15. d	16. a	17. c	18. d	19. c	20. a
21. a	22. d	23. a	24. b	25. b	26. d				

Chapter 7

1. a	2. c	3. d	4. d	5. d	6. c	7. b	8. b	9. d	10. c
11. b	12. b	13. d	14. d	15. a					

Chapter 8

1. a	2. d	3. a	4. d	5. b	6. d	7. b	8. a	9. d	10. d
11. d	12. a	13. b	14. d	15. c	16. d	17. d	18. c	19. b	20. d
21. b	22. a	23. b	24. d	25. d	26. d	27. d	28. c	29. b	

Chapter 9

1. d	2. d	3. d	4. a	5. d	6. d	7. c	8. a	9. d	10. d
11. d	12. a	13. a	14. d	15. b	16. d	17. d	18. c	19. d	20. b
21. a	22. d	23. d	24. d	25. d	26. d	27. d	28. d	29. b	

Chapter 10

1. b	2. d	3. b	4. d	5. d	6. d	7. b	8. c	9. d	10. d
11. d	12. c	13. d	14. d	15. c					

ANSWER KEY

Chapter 11
1. b   2. d   3. b   4. d   5. d   6. d   7. b   8. d   9. d   10. d
11. a   12. a   13. d   14. d   15. d   16. c   17. d   18. d   19. c

Chapter 12
1. d   2. d   3. d   4. b   5. d   6. c   7. d   8. b   9. d   10. d
11. b   12. b   13. d   14. d   15. b   16. d   17. b   18. c   19. d   20. d
21. d   22. b

Chapter 13
1. b   2. c   3. c   4. a   5. d   6. d   7. d   8. a   9. d   10. d
11. d   12. d   13. d   14. d   15. d   16. d   17. d   18. a   19. d   20. b

Chapter 14
1. d   2. b   3. b   4. b   5. a   6. c   7. b   8. a   9. d   10. b
11. d   12. d   13. a   14. a   15. d   16. d   17. c   18. d   19. d   20. d
21. d   22. d   23. d   24. d   25. a   26. a   27. b

Chapter 15
1. d   2. a   3. d   4. b   5. d   6. a   7. d   8. a   9. d   10. d
11. a   12. c   13. d   14. c   15. d   16. c   17. d   18. c   19. a   20. d

Chapter 16
1. d   2. d   3. b   4. d   5. d   6. d   7. b   8. b   9. d   10. d
11. c   12. d   13. b   14. d   15. a   16. d   17. c   18. d   19. d   20. b
21. b

Chapter 17
1. a   2. a   3. b   4. c   5. a   6. b   7. d   8. d   9. d   10. d
11. b   12. d   13. a   14. b   15. c   16. c   17. b   18. d   19. d   20. d
21. d   22. d   23. d